DYSLEXIA AND COLLEGE SUCCESS
by Maria S.E. Johnson and James Nuttall

CHAPTER 1 - Introduction

Sharing Lessons From Life

Hello, we are James Nuttall, Ph.D. and Maria Johnson, B.A.. We wish to welcome you to this book on helping the college student with dyslexia. We wrote this book since we are dyslexic and loved going to college. To differentiate between the two narrators, any important shift in who is writing will be indicated. So when Dr. Nuttall writes about himself he will say "I, Jim." If Maria writes about herself she will say "I, Maria." When referring to each other we will simply use our names "Jim" or "Maria."

While growing up, I, Jim, knew that I had a reading problem. During elementary school and high school, I struggled to read. Throughout school, I was basically a non-reader. Every day, I watched my family and fellow students read books, magazines, and newspapers. I longed to do the same. When I went away to college, I visited the University of Chicago Reading Clinic where I learned that I had dyslexia. I persevered with college and eventually earned a Ph.D. in Psychology from Michigan State University. I asked Maria to join me in writing this book since she is a successful student and her college experiences are current and up-to-date.

I, Maria, have always struggled to read. I considered myself a non-reader and acted like one for most of my life. I love history, though, so I learned about history through listening to people and watching documentaries rather than reading. I started college at a very young age and carried on until recently, receiving my B.A. in Humanities and Cultural Studies from the University of South Florida. I found out in the last year of my college career that I had dyslexia and was formally diagnosed after graduating. Despite my late diagnosis, I always knew I could not read well and developed ways to help myself do my best despite my difficulties.

This book is aimed at struggling readers and writers, suggesting to them ways to succeed at college. Over the years we learned some tricks for coping with dyslexia, many of which are enhanced by recent technologies. We would like to pass these tricks on to you. If you struggle with reading and writing, we hope you will find this book helpful. You do not need to read this book from front to back, but can skip around, reading what you like and find useful.

Why This Book?

As we grew up, we struggled with reading and writing. When we went to college these difficulties did not go away. In fact, the work demands of college exacerbated these struggles. Even though our colleges were nurturing, there were few people to talk with to get advice and help about our struggles. So for the most part we forged our own pathways to success. We thought it would be beneficial to put some of our experiences and lessons learned down on paper. Hopefully, by doing so we can help others who struggle with reading and writing find success. In this book we outline how technology and study strategies can revolutionize the lives of college students with dyslexia. Along the way, we discuss a variety of techniques to improve the reading and writing skills of people who have dyslexia. We hope you enjoy this book, and feel free to email us at nuttall.james@gmail.com.

CHAPTER 2 - What Is Dyslexia?

What is Dyslexia?

The primary indication of dyslexia is a difficulty with reading and spelling. Some reading difficulties could result from lack of adequate instruction, practice, or availability of books. Dyslexia, however, is not a result of these factors. Evidence shows that dyslexia is a neurological learning difference, based on differences in how the brain processes print and language. Let's look at how dyslexia affects Bill, a college sophomore. Bill is a smart, friendly student, and loves sports. But Bill has difficulty with reading.

Phonological Awareness

Bill has difficulty hearing and pronouncing the sounds of new words that his professors say in their lectures. This is especially true of scientific terms.

Phonics

Bill has a hard time sounding out long words or scientific terms he meets in his textbooks.

Sequential Short-term Memory

Bill often cannot remember sequences of letters. When trying to copy words from PowerPoint slides during lectures, he can only remember about three letters at a time. He has to keep looking at the slides frequently while trying to copy words.

Auditory Memory

Bill has a hard time remembering names or numbers as they are said to him. While in class, if he asks a girl her name, he cannot remember it unless he quickly writes it down. The same holds true for phone numbers.

Verbal Memory

While reading complex sentences, Bill often cannot remember all the words in a sentence as he reads, so he has to reread the sentence several times to understand it.

Overworked Short-term Memory

When we perform a task like reading, we use our short-term memory to keep the words in our mind, so we can make sense of what we are reading. At times Bill is working so hard to read each word that he often looses his place while reading. His working memory is so focused on the words that by the end of the paragraph he has no idea what he has read.

Verbal Processing

It is hard for Bill to keep the different steps of directions in his mind. So while the professor solves a mathematical equation Bill looses track of the different steps in the solution.

Rapid Naming Speed

Research shows that students like Bill recall words more slowly than others. So Bill takes longer to recognize words and remember words as he reads. Bill reads more slowly than most of his friends. It takes him much longer to read assignments.

Automatic Word Recognition

Proficient readers automatically recognize words quickly. It may take only up to 12 times of seeing a new word to make it automatic both in terms of recognition and memory. However, for Bill it takes 30 or more times to learn new words, so learning new English or foreign language vocabulary is an arduous process.

Subvocalization

Bill does not automatically recognize words silently. Instead, while reading Bill says each word to himself quietly, so his reading is much slower than the other students who are true silent readers. A friend suggested that Bill put a pencil between his teeth to stop saying the words. When Bill tried this he got very frustrated and stopped reading. This trick did not work for Bill. In fact, this is a bad strategy often improperly recommended to dyslexic readers.

Spelling and Writing

Bill has a rich vocabulary. When he speaks with others, they are impressed with his erudition. When he writes, though, his vocabulary is stunted in comparison to his speech. Bill uses only the words that he can spell, so his writing often does not show what he knows.

Inability to Follow Printed Text

Bill keeps his finger on his place in the text as he reads. Otherwise, he often loses his place.

The Dyslexic Struggle

As can be seen, dyslexia affects more than just the reading process. Individuals with dyslexia often have difficulty with organizing assignments and remembering important dates for tests. They may also have difficulty with doing calculations in one's head as opposed to doing them on paper. I, Jim, was the last one in my class to learn the multiplication tables. Then sometimes while speaking, your mind simply goes blank, giving no indication of what the train of conversation was about. A very frequent characteristic of dyslexia is having a problem with short term memory. As pointed out above, this leads to struggling with learning people's names or looking up and dialing phone numbers. Finally, the emotional stress of living with dyslexia is potent, though often not discussed. After years of struggling with reading and school assignments, it is not unusual to have a very low self-image and to lack self-confidence. On the positive-side, every person has strengths to draw on. Often individuals with dyslexia have learned to be persistent and self motivated.

We know that 25% to 30% of high school students struggle with reading. Generally 10% of students struggle to such a degree that they can be considered dyslexic. Men and women are equally affected. Additionally, dyslexia runs in families. Often, a mother or father also struggled as a reader in school. In the early grades, dyslexic children have a hard time learning to read. Later on in high school, dyslexic students can read, but often very slowly and with great difficulty.

Elementary to High School

Both children and adults can struggle with reading. Ben, who is a third grader, has a very difficult time sounding out words. Sue is in fourth grade and often sees words but does not know what they mean. Richie is in seventh grade and reads all of the words but does not understand the sentences. Kelley, a ninth grader, gets discouraged about doing homework. Her reading is so slow, the homework takes hours while her friends get done fast. Guy is an eleventh grader, but is reading at a fifth grade level. He is unable to read his high school textbooks. These struggles give a picture of what dyslexia looks like for different people.

Key Areas

The key areas of reading are word decoding, vocabulary knowledge, comprehension of sentences, fluency while reading, acquiring adequate background knowledge, and finding the appropriate book to read.

Decoding

The ability to sound out and blend words is basic to the process of reading. At the very beginning, all readers must learn how to "decode" words. Phonics teaches the sounds that go with letters and letter combinations. When adults are having decoding difficulties, often one-on-one tutoring with a multi-sensory approach to learning phonics will help. Older struggling readers, especially those with dyslexia, have difficulty with decoding and phonics. It is not unusual for dyslexic adults to still struggle to figure out the words that they see. Sometimes participating in an adult literacy program of tutoring at a dyslexic center can help.

Vocabulary

Almost every new book contains new words. One of the major tasks of the college student is the learning of a large quantity of new vocabulary associated with each subject area being studied.

Fluency

Kelley, a college junior, reads slowly and stumbles over words. Kelley reads haltingly and with little expression in his voice. Often he must reread texts to develop fluency in a subject area.

Comprehension and Background Knowledge

College textbooks and resource materials are often difficult to comprehend. There are two ways to help with comprehension. First, you can read the chapter several times. Many times we do not understand the textbook chapters the first time around. Second, gain background knowledge outside of your current reading. When you do not have the background knowledge in a subject, the subject does not make sense. In order to get the background knowledge needed for understanding, it is helpful to first read an easier secondary book to get some information. There are a number of these types of books for most college subjects.

Reading and the Brain

Reading involves a number of major systems of the brain. The first area, of course, is our visual system. We first must see the letters and words on a page with our eyes. The images of the letters fall onto our retinas, but the letters do not go like a picture to our brains. Instead, the cells in our retinas actually respond to the lines and curves of each letter. Our retinal cells fire, sending information about the lines and curves to the back of our brains where the visual cortex is located in the occipital lobe (see Figure 1). As we repeatedly see the angles, curves and lines of the letters, our brains learn these neural patterns and soon learn to recognize letters and words.

As we read, our eyes actually move in small steps across a line of print. These movements are called saccades. After each time we move our eyes, we stop with a fixation and focus on the letters in the line. Our eyes can clearly see only about six to eight letters in each fixation. This is often enough to see a word or two. Non-dyslexic readers often experience their eyes easily gliding along the line and taking in the print. But dyslexic readers frequently have to use a lot of attention to make their eyes move from one spot to the next. Dyslexic readers find that their eyes often back up to reexamine what they have seen, so reading is jumpy and slower.

There are two major areas for language in our brains that are used while we read. For most people, these areas are on the left side of the brain. About 95% of right-handers have language predominantly on the left side. Left-handers are more mixed, 18% with language on the right side and almost 20% with language on both the right and left sides of the brain. No one knows exactly why these differences occur. There is no difference in language proficiency for right or left-handers.

Parts of the Human Brain

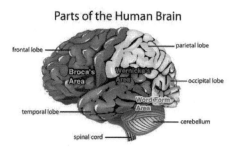

One major language area — Broca's Area — is located about where your left temple is located. This area is important for speaking. It organizes the phonemes of a word that we want to say and arranges the words into proper grammatical order. Wernicke's Area, a second language area, is located a little higher than your temple but behind your left ear. Wernicke's Area is very important in understanding the meaning of words. We need to understand the meanings of words both when we hear them and when we speak them. These two areas of the brain are connected by a major network of nerve fibers, since they coordinate both our listening to and production of speech. As we learn to read, our brains learn to make connections between the visual system, seeing words, and these language systems of our brain.

Additionally, reading activates our memories of what we know, our emotional reactions to things, and our experiences of colors, sounds, and movement. We often create internal images of what we are reading. For adults, these systems coordinate efficiently and effectively. In our adult brain, years of practice have created neurological connections between these systems. As we learn to read, the required neurological connections are created between these various systems.

Dr. Sally Shaywitz, M.D., the director of the Yale Center for Dyslexia and Creativity, specializes in research on dyslexia and reading. She studies how the brain processes reading. Dr. Shaywitz places individuals in a functional magnetic resonance imaging (fMRI) machine and asks them to read text projected on a screen. Using the fMRI she scans the brain. These scans map out the brain's activity while the person reads. Her work shows that there are three primary areas in the brain which are activated during reading.

The first area for reading is Broca's Area. Again, Broca's Area is important in understanding the phonemes associated with letters—speech sounds and the grammar of sentences. This frontal area is pictured in Figure 1. In reading, decoding letters is associated with matching speech sounds to the letters. This is called the phonological pathway to reading. In this pathway the phonemes are combined to make words. The second area, Wernicke's Area, is related to analyzing word parts, syllables, prefixes and suffixes. Most importantly, this area also attaches meaning to the words we decipher. For example, if this area is damaged, we can see and say words, but we do not know what the words mean. This second part to reading is known as the semantic (meaning) pathway to reading. The third important area for reading is located in an area overlapping both the visual and the auditory cortex. This is the "Word Form Area." In highly effective readers this area governs the automatic reading process. When reading is automatic, words are recognized quickly and often silently.

The fMRI studies show that all three areas are used by non-dyslexic readers while reading. As a person gets better at reading, the two back areas are used more and more. The fMRI images of dyslexic readers show a different pattern. Dyslexic readers show a high level of activity in the front, Broca's Area. The two back areas are not used as much. Both adults and children with dyslexia have a greater reliance on the phonological pathway to reading. Dyslexic readers primarily use sounding out words and often speaking words aloud in order to read. By not using the word analysis and rapid analysis areas (semantic pathway), dyslexic readers are slower readers. Some research shows that early systematic reading instruction for dyslexic children can increase the use of the word analytic and rapid analysis areas of the brain. Dr. Shaywitz's book *Overcoming Dyslexia: A New and Complete Science-Based Program for Reading Problems at Any Level* talks about her research and how early intervention for dyslexic children can help wire their brains for reading.

Getting a Diagnosis

You might ask yourself, "Why should I get an evaluation for dyslexia?" An evaluation can answer questions you have about your reading and your struggles with assignments. A diagnosis of dyslexia can open the possibility of reasonable accommodations to help you succeed. For example, you can have extra time when taking tests. It has been shown that when dyslexic students are given extra time on tests their performance is greatly improved. However, giving non-dyslexic students extra time does not change their test scores. Thus, accommodations do not amount to receiving an unfair advantage. Accommodations help to equalize the playing field for students with dyslexia.

When you get evaluated this often helps you overcome negative self-images. Over the years you may have heard others tell you to simply "try harder" or "stop goofing off." You may have come to believe such evaluations of yourself. An honest evaluation of your skills and potential can help you defeat the negative images that you have incorporated into your self-concept (or image). You may also have come to believe that if you could just work hard enough or move to a new college and start fresh, your difficulties would disappear. An evaluation can point out your strengths and help with accommodations, which is like getting a fresh start. A good evaluation will help you understand yourself better.

If you think that you have dyslexia, it is important to get tested for it. Here are several checklists as a starting point for investigating dyslexia. The first checklist is provided by the International Dyslexia Association: http://www.interdys.org/AreYouDyslexic_AdultTest.htm. A score of 7 or more is indicative of dyslexia.

1. Do you read slowly?

2. Did you have trouble learning how to read when you were in school?

3. Do you often have to read something two or three times before it makes sense?

4. Are you uncomfortable reading out loud?

5. Do you omit, transpose, or add letters when you are reading or writing?

6. Do you find you still have spelling mistakes in your writing even after Spell Check?
7. Do you find it difficult to pronounce uncommon multi-syllable words when you are reading?
8. Do you choose to read magazines or short articles rather than longer books and novels?
9. When you were in school, did you find it extremely difficult to learn a foreign language?
10. Do you avoid work projects or courses that require extensive reading?

Here is another helpful checklist:
http://www.xtraordinarypeople.com/x-factor/
1. Do you find difficulty telling left from right?
2. Is map reading or finding your way to a strange place confusing?
3. Do you dislike reading aloud?
4. Do you take longer that you should to read a page of a book?
5. Do you find it difficult to remember the sense of what you have read?
6. Do you dislike reading long books?
7. Is your spelling poor?
8. Is your writing difficult to read?
9. Do you get confused if you have to speak in public?
10. Do you find it difficult to take messages on the telephone and pass them on correctly?

11. When you have to say a long word, do you sometimes find it difficult to get all the sounds in the right order?

12. Do you find it difficult to do sums in your head without using your fingers or paper?

13. When using the telephone, do you tend to get the numbers mixed up when you dial?

14. Do you find it difficult to say the months of the year forwards in a fluent manner?

15. Do you find it difficult to say the months of the year backwards?

16. Do you mix up dates and times and miss appointments?

17. When writing cheques do you frequently find yourself making mistakes?

18. Do you find forms difficult and confusing?

19. Do you mix up bus numbers like 95 and 59?

20. Did you find it hard to learn your multiplication tables at school?

The 12 questions which were the strongest indicators of dyslexia were as follows (Importance - Question):

1st - Question 17
2nd - Question 13
3rd - Question 7
4th - Question16
5th - Question 18
6th - Question 10

7th - Question 19
8th - Question 14
9th - Question 20
10th - Question 4
11th - Question 1
12th - Question 11

A score of 9 or more is a strong indication of dyslexia. Checklist devised by Michael Vinegrad: A Revised Dyslexia Checklist. Educare, No 48 March 1994.

The Evaluation

Usually a neuropsychologist who specializes in comprehensive neuropsychological evaluations for dyslexia does the evaluation. Often the evaluation may also include an educational specialist with knowledge of reading and writing tests. The evaluation begins with an interview gathering information about your medical history and why you are seeking an evaluation. There may be questions about your family history, such as did any of your relatives struggle with reading and spelling, since dyslexia often runs in families. You will most likely be asked about your school experiences, like when did you struggle with reading; do you have difficulty remembering things and do you have difficulties with writing.

There will be a series of tests, which may take three hours or so. Often a psychologist will give you a test of general intelligence. This test has a number of sub-tests. These are broken down into verbal tests and performance non-verbal tests. Even though you have dyslexia, you will be surprised at how well you do. So many students with dyslexia say they know they should do better but feel stupid. This intelligence test often shows just the opposite. Your difficulties are caused by reading problems, and you are actually just as smart as everyone else.

There are often reading and writing evaluations. Reading evaluations cover both silent and oral reading. The reading tests may also include reading what are called "nonsense" words. These are letter combinations that sound just like regular words but ones you have never seen before. There will probably be a test on spelling. You may think, "Well I'm not good at those things." Do not worry. These tests will show how you are doing in order to help you succeed in college and at work.

Where can you get a diagnosis? You may live in a community that has a center for dyslexia. At these centers they frequently test for dyslexia and also offer special instruction in reading. In larger cities you can google "neuropsychologist" to locate an evaluator. Also university centers which train neuropsychologists can provide evaluations. An evaluation must be done by a licensed neuropsychologist in order to make sure you qualify for university disability services or for accommodations from your employer. Remember the biggest thing you will receive from an evaluation is a greater understanding of yourself.

Jim's Evaluation

When I went away to the university, I found that I could not do the reading by myself. I could read only about four or five pages in an hour, so I quickly arranged to have other students read my textbooks to me. I wanted to improve my reading, since my reading was so horrendously slow. I figured if that if I could get the right reading instruction then I would read like everyone else. I arranged to visit the University of Chicago Reading Clinic for a diagnostic workup, hoping that this clinic could improve my reading. I simply wanted to read quickly and fluently and understand my assignments, just as other students did. Here is the story of my trip to this clinic.

University Book Store—a Closed Book to Me:

The books at the University of Chicago bookstore looked like gemstones with their red, green, black, and blue covers. They lay in orderly stacks on the white metal shelves under the bright fluorescent lights. Few took notice of me that day, a pale thin young man with thick glasses and black hair. Everyone's attention was focused outside on the sunny spring day and the lines of graduates in their plump reddish robes. Proud parents and excited college students waited for the ceremony to mark the completion of an education at one of America's most prestigious universities. In the graduation line stood a large number of young adults with robes having three stripes on the arms, signifying their Ph.D.s, Doctors of Philosophy, of Science, of Knowledge.

Knowledge Everywhere But Out of My Reach:
I did not spend my time looking at the line of graduating students. Instead, I moved in a trance up and down the aisles of the bookstore, picking up one book and then another. My hands and my heart molded themselves around each book, feeling its size, its weight, its thickness and sensing its importance. Each book was a treasure. In an awe-filled voice, I slowly sounded out the titles: College Grammar, Calculus, Human Anatomy and Physiology, The History of the Middle Ages, Anthology of English Literature, Fluid Mechanics, Business Law... on and on and on. The titles both excited and overwhelmed me, numbing my mind. Books, knowledge, all were closed to me, placed outside of my ability to read them.

The Reading Clinic:
The time came to go back across the tree-lined campus to the University of Chicago Reading Clinic for the rest of my evaluation. I sat in front of a large machine with words projected on a screen. I read each line as the machine photographed my eye movements. I became aware of how frightfully often my eyes went backwards

instead of forwards. With all my might I tried to make my wandering eyes go forward. But neither my eyes nor my brain would obey my will. A great sense of relief came over me when the test ended.

Then the examiner and I sat at a small table. In front of me, he placed tiles with symbols: a star, a square, a circle, a triangle. He started with only two or three in a line. Mixing them up, he asked me to place them back in the correct order. Then he lined up four... five...six...seven...eight. There were pictures to place in sequence and block designs to make sense of. This part of the test seemed fun and unrelated to my reading problems. As we finished I asked, "What's this test called." "The Illinois Psycholinguistics Test," he replied. "We can tell how you process information with this test."

Struggling to Read the Words:

Inevitably there were paragraphs of words to read aloud. Aware that I stumbled and stopped at each word, I prayed for smoothness to come to my speech. As a young man of twenty, I was filled with anxiety. I struggled to sound out the simplest of words. The examiner recorded my voice as I read. I stumbled over words, repeated words and skipped words. Finally, tears of frustration, embarrassment and longing flowed down my cheeks. The examiner stopped the recording and put his hand on my shoulder. "That's O.K., we can stop now. I think I've got enough material to do my evaluation report." "How soon will the report be done?" I asked. "Several weeks from now. I will mail you a copy at your home." With that we parted and I took the long train ride back to Indiana and my university dorm room.

The Report Arrives:

The clinical report was long and complex. So, I asked my mother to read the report, saying, "I wanted to go to this clinic and get help with my reading. I can't get through college without being able to read better." She and my father spent the next day with the report. Then, they called me in to talk to me. They read sections of the report to me, especially emphasizing the part of the letter and report which stated that the clinic could not help me. I had something called dyslexia. The report concluded, "Since you seem to learn and pass your classes using readers, we strongly support your continued use of readers in pursuing your education."

I was devastated. I took the report and went to my room. Sitting on my bed with tears welling up in my eyes, I struggled for hours through every line of it, hoping to find the answer for a cure to my reading problems. Couldn't anybody fix me? Couldn't someone, somewhere, teach me to read better—to read faster? These questions with no answers swirled in my head. I felt dizzy and heartsick. I just wanted to be like the other students, to read as they read. If I could read well, surely I could pass my classes. Reading faster was the key to becoming a computer programmer or a biology teacher. Reading held out so many possibilities. But all of these possibilities seemed out of my reach. I could not read the required books. For me the most memorable paragraph of the report was on my "Reading Achievement." After two years at the university, my reading test indicated that I only read at the third grade level. That, and the words "we can do nothing for you" created a deep pain that shocked me from head to toe.

Using Accommodations:

The major thing that stood out for me during my testing was how often my eyes back tracked instead of moving forward while trying to read. Even though I was heartsick at first that the University Clinic could not fix my reading problems, I accepted accommodations and learned new ways to succeed. I returned to my university in the fall armed with a new tape recorder. I recorded my readers as they read to me. As they read aloud, I would follow along. I would also follow along when rereading every chapter of my assignments. My readers read my books, my class notes, my underlinings, and supplementary materials. My grades moved from D's to C's to B's and eventually to A's. I could take only half the credit load others took, but I was succeeding!

If you are told to "simply try harder" or to "study harder," this will not solve the problem with reading. Overcoming the barriers and coping are very challenging.

It is correct to tell someone with dyslexia that learning can be hard work. Real learning is not easy. Additionally, adults with dyslexia will need others to give them help in learning. You should not be afraid to ask for help. When I entered college, reading at the third grade level, I wasn't lazy. I was unprepared and needed accommodations. My journey has been a tumultuous struggle from illiteracy to literacy. I could not read the college texts, I could not write in complete sentences, and 30% of what I wrote was misspelled. I had all of my undergraduate and graduate books either read to me or on audiotape. This "Reading To Me" and "Following Along" experience opened up books and knowledge to me. I completed my college degree, a master's degree and finally a Doctor of Philosophy in Psychology. Dyslexia sets up real barriers to learning, but books can be read by using readers, audiobooks, computers, or an iPad. When you get an evaluation and accommodations, you too can succeed at the university.

Maria's Evaluation

I grew up knowing exactly why others thought I could not read well. Set backs in the first four years of my life —not being read to and not crawling (I spent the first years of my life in an orphanage in Russia, and have a physical disability called Arthrogryposis Multiplex Congenita) — were still exerting influence into my teen years. I knew that reading was very taxing and slow regardless of how hard I tried, and that I could not comprehend what I read well. I accepted that I would get headaches or be mentally tired a lot. I would have to reject doing a reading assignment or postpone a writing assignment due to my mental exhaustion from readings earlier that day. This was all I had ever known. I would often hope that one day I would just miraculously read fluently and well. I would even buy books for when I could read. I would buy a book and get so excited, but then it would have to sit on a shelf until that miraculous day came. Throughout college I faced my difficulties with a cheerful attitude: I told myself "one day you will be able to read like everyone else." It was a weird world I lived in, with both struggle and naive overzealous hope.

The May after my second year of University I went to a friend's graduation party. I mingled around and found my parents talking with a lady. I was surprised to hear my parents talking about my reading issues — we do not talk about that! They defended themselves by saying that this lady was a reading teacher. Feeling more comfortable, I allowed myself to open up a little bit. I told her that when I look at a book it is like a sea of letters…I read one word at a time and often find myself confused about what I just read and having lost my spot on the page. She said I could very well have "dyslexia!" I was shocked and taken aback — after all, up until then no one had suggested that as a possibility. I went home and started researching Dyslexia. I took a number of online tests and every one came back saying that there was a very good chance that I was dyslexic. Learning about what dyslexia is led me to discover that I fit that mold well.

I had three reactions to the news that I had a legitimate learning disability. One, I felt such relief to know it was not just me nor was it just my life circumstance. I had a distinct neurological difference that caused me to read differently than most. Two, when I read about others' experience with dyslexia I found myself numb, for they articulated what I had experienced for years. I thought I was alone and here was a community of people that had my same struggles ten or twenty times over. The shock of that realization was difficult at first but it became a blessing with time. Three, I was devastated beyond belief that I would not, one day, miraculously be able to read on my own. Everything that was hard for me would stay hard for me. I doubted everything and felt a compulsion to find some mindless path that would not require reading. I did not let this attitude remain. I held firm to my passion for Medieval literature and resolved to seek out ways to help my Dyslexia.

After I initially found out about Dyslexia, I mostly put it aside and finished my last year of University. After graduating, I had the time to truly dedicate myself to lessening the crutch of my Dyslexia. I am happy to say I found multiple ways to help me read and write my best, many of which are in this book, so I will not spoil the surprise here. Now armed with life-changing tools, I felt I could start telling some friends and family, whom I had kept in the dark, about my Dyslexia. After a few conversations I felt a strong sense that I needed to be formally evaluated. I knew I wanted to apply to graduate school, so I would have to take the GRE. I needed to have proof of my Dyslexia to receive the accommodations that would help me test well. Also, I knew at my next school I would tell the professors from the beginning that I had Dyslexia and that they may want to see the proof. Most importantly, I needed to know for sure myself — to have that confirmation of my diagnosis in black and white.

I went to a Psychologist. To begin, I told her my life story, focusing on my scholastic development and education. Additionally, I described in detail my reading and writing experiences. Then I took an intelligence test. After the intelligence test I began the achievement test. I did many small tests, each to determine something about how I read and wrote.

One test had me pronouncing words. Once the words became long and unfamiliar I started to be unintentionally comical in my pronunciation. Later on, I was told that when I read an unfamiliar word I had the habit of either adding or omitting letters and syllables.

Another reading test seemed on the surface very easy but actually ended up showing my difficulties the most. I had to read just two to four sentences and answer a yes or no question about the paragraph. I was supposed to do as many as I could in the time given. I read the mini-paragraph. Then I questioned myself what the beginning said once I finished reading the end, so I re-read the paragraph. I started my sentence well but my eyes, without provocation, moved down to the next line before I had finished the last sentence. Thus, my sentence would read something like: the cat loves he went. So I read the paragraph a third time, this time straining myself not to miss any words or let my eyes wander. I had to read each paragraph two to three times to answer the question. My test score resonated with these difficulties and my slowness: I was dramatically below average in my reading comprehension.

I recall one writing test was as painful as it was long. I was given two sentences and asked to write the sentence in the middle to finalize the paragraph. At first, I had all these ideas about what I wanted to say and how I wanted to emulate the fine style of the original writer. However, when it came time for me to physically write the sentence I could not get myself to express any of the good ideas I had — maybe because I could not spell a word I wanted to use or because I did not know if I could use the right grammatical structure for what I wanted to say. I ended up writing a simple and extremely short sentence devoid of the eloquence I had originally intended.

These two tests along with a host of others told me that I was very dyslexic. They also said, though, that I had dysgraphia. At the age of twenty, I finally knew why I persistently struggled to read.

There are a few very positive things that have come from my diagnosis of Dyslexia. Other than just knowing why reading and writing are difficult for me, I know that I can obtain help to read and write better. If I make the needed lifestyle changes I can improve my reading and writing ability. Most significantly, my old life is gone! I do not have to skip required readings or have to read things by myself without help. I can get less headaches and do more.

It is worth getting evaluated because it opens doors. You can find other ways to do things. With the official evaluation you can get memberships to Learning Ally and Bookshare. You can also get accommodations at a College or University. Learning I was dyslexic proved to be one of the most trying moments in my life, yet at the same time one of the best motivators to learn how to read and write without struggle!

CHAPTER 3 - Struggling with Dyslexia

Jim's experience

I, Jim, have limited vision. As a child I held my books just a few inches from my face while reading. Most teachers and individuals assumed that my great difficulty with reading was due to my poor vision. But I knew people with vision much worse then mine who could read just fine. In the first 12 grades of school, I rarely read anything. In the first five grades, I was oblivious to the fact that I was doing anything differently than my fellow students. I spent much of my time daydreaming and thinking about not being in school. I love riding horses, so I often imagined myself riding horses in the Colorado Rocky Mountains.

I first became aware of my difficulties while in middle school. During sixth grade English, we were working on improving our reading speeds. We had a special book with short, timed reading exercises. Each reading was timed in order for us to calculate our reading speeds. On the first day, I remember trying to read to the best of my ability. Like the other students, I counted up the number of words that I read and divided by the time spent reading. This gave us our reading speed in words read per minute. We each announced the number of words per minute read. I read 27 words per minute. The student sitting next to me read 350 words per minute. My teacher then said, "Now in the next reading pull out all of the stops and read as fast as you can." I figured this was my opportunity to shine, so I read as fast as I could. The student sitting next to me now read 600 words per minute. I anxiously calculated my reading speed. I read 33 words per minute. I had gained only five words per minute. All I could do was sit in despair and cry. I finally knew something was dreadfully wrong with my performance in school. To this day I remember this event with great heartache. To help you understand how catastrophic my reading was, here are the typical reading speeds for elementary students.

Reading Fluency in words per minute:
    First grade – 60
    Second grade – 70
    Third grade – 90
    Fourth grade – 120
    Fifth grade – 150

Thus, in sixth grade, I was functioning at half of what a typical first grader could do. In school my classmates and I were given copious amounts of homework with lots of reading. I was totally unable to do this reading. So, at night I would sit in my room sharpening my pencils, arranging my papers and otherwise trying to avoid the reading. I usually got very little done and had nothing to turn in the next day. To get by, I would ask my friends what they had read and what they had learned. These updates kept me going in class. This strategy for learning is now given the name "peer buddies."

    I especially listened closely in class. On my tests I would write down what I remember my teachers saying. Nowadays if your college will allow it, you can actually record the lectures using a device called the Live Scribe Pen. The Live Scribe Pen is able to sync your hand written notes with the audio portions of a lecture. Also, iPad apps like *Notability* can sync notes with the recorded lectures.

Going to College

Even though I was a non-reader throughout high school, both my parents, who had college degrees, and I expected that I would go to college. As a senior in high school I took the SAT. During the test my reading rate was very slow. I remember scoring in the 7th percentile on the test. This means 93% of those taking the test scored above my score. Fortunately, the college where I applied accepted me. As I left for college my father said that I would need recorded textbooks and have other students to read to me. Everyone, except me, still believed my reading problems were due to my visual difficulties.

I have gotten every possible grade one can get in college: A, B, C, D, F, I for Incomplete and W for Withdrawal. Yes, I was not always an 'A' student! Needless to say I had to learn a lot about how to read and how to study. First of all, I had to have everything read to me. I had most of my books recorded for me by Learning Ally to create my audio-supported reading. Learning Ally no longer records all books sent to them. One must request that books be recorded. Some will and some will not be recorded. Today, I get most of my digitized books from Bookshare and use my iPad to read these books.

When I started college I tried to do my reading on my own. My reading speed was extremely slow. Professors would give a 30 page reading assignment per class. I found that I could only read 5 pages in an hour. It became obvious that I could not do the reading by myself. I started using recorded textbooks and student readers to assist with the reading. I call this reading "audio-supported reading." With audio-supported reading I could read 20 pages in an hour.

Writing was also a problem. When I went to the University, I was an extremely poor speller and writer. I remember sitting at the cashier's table filling out my first check for tuition. The person at the desk said I had to pay $650. I asked, "How do you spell University?" "How do you spell hundred?" "How do you spell fifty?" This experience showed that, as a dyslexic student, I was in serious trouble.

In Freshman Composition 75% of my sentences were actually incomplete. An incomplete sentence is only a phrase or fragment of a real sentence. My papers were also peppered with misspelled words. When I took my first semester in-class final, my essay had more than 50 misspelled words. Fortunately, I had a very understanding English professor who passed me in spite of these problems. According to English Department guidelines, she should have failed my test. I believe she could see that I was a student with potential and supported my attempts at writing.

Maria's experience

I, Maria, was born in 1994 in Stavropol, Russia. Within three weeks of my birth I was handed over to an orphanage in Stavropol. I remained there until I was 3 1/2 years old. In the orphanage I was given a comfortable place to live, toys, and children to play with, but no early education. I was not read to. I was not taught my letters, albeit Russian letters. I was not introduced to numbers.

I was born with a physical disability called Arthrogryposis Multiplex Congenita. This condition affects the movement of my joints and muscle strength. My hands are crooked down. My knees do not bend fully. Before having surgery, I walked on my toes instead of my heels. I am straight-legged and straight-armed in the truest sense. As a baby I did not crawl. I immediately jumped to walking. Some individuals have attributed my bypassing crawling to my difficulty in reading.

When I was 3 1/2 years old I was adopted by a loving couple from Alabama. They were not held back by my physical disability, developmental delays, or the fact I spoke no English. Therefore, I came to the USA in 1998. In the beginning I just spoke or sang in Russian non-stop. At first my parents thought it would be beneficial to put me in a school for the developmentally delayed. However, I showed an ability to learn English quickly and well, so they chose to put me in a traditional early education school.

First grade was a very significant time for me. Halfway through the school year, my parents were urged to hold me back a grade because I demonstrated severe difficulties with reading. At the time, everyone blamed my lack of crawling as a baby, stunted education in the orphanage, and the fact I learned English at four as a second language. This explanation satisfied everyone and I was held back a grade.

After completing kindergarten again, my parents chose to move me to a different school. Unfortunately, my issues traveled with me! I remember very well we were working on reading in the class and each student had to go to the teacher's desk and read a small paperback book of just a few pages. The teacher did the traditional things of helping the young student sound out the words and encouraging them to read on their own. It felt like I spent hours at her desk on just one page. I would sound out each letter and then not be able to say the word. I would do this over and over. This is the first moment I can remember that I knew reading was not just hard but practically impossible.

Starting in fourth grade I became homeschooled. Homeschooling really worked for me because I am a self-driven person and can thrive on my own schedule. I came to love history and it played a major role in my scholastic schedule. However, I could only read the most basic history books. So I watched documentaries and listened closely when adults talked about history. Knowing that I could not go "read it later" forced me to develop a good oral memory to enable me to learn what I wanted to. Even though I could learn by listening, I still consistently faced my reading difficulties. Even up to the age of 13 I could only read with ease very simple books.

I remember that when I was 11, I wanted to go to Space Camp in Huntsville, Alabama. To raise the money,I said that I would read ten books in a month. I knew that I could do this because I had recently found a series called *The Boxcar Kids* that I not only enjoyed but could read! The books had large fonts and the lines were spaced dramatically so it felt like I read a lot when I only read a little bit. I noticed when I looked at the shelf that some of the books in the series had smaller fonts and more words. I remember feeling, when I saw those books, that I could never read them. It was like a brick wall in my way.

Despite my inability to read difficult books, I still read enough easy books that enabled me to actually learn to read. When I read, I just did it very slowly and I always would say the words as I read them. When I tried to remember something I read, though, it felt like remembering a dream. I could recall one paragraph really well, but then I would completely black-out on two or three paragraphs worth of information, only to then remember some specific sentence really well later on. Even now, whenever I read a sentence or a paragraph or a book I suffer from the "Swiss cheese effect." The things I remember I understand, but I black-out often on other parts. To combat this, I make notes in excruciating detail. I don't allow myself to move on without capturing the essence of what I just read so that I won't later have to depend on my memory.

Between fourth and eighth grade, I read what I needed to, avoided reading what I didn't need to, and compensated for all the readings I could not do by listening and over-thinking. In ninth grade, I was given the opportunity to go to community college and take classes for free while still being in high school — in other words to be dual-enrolled. For each class I took I would get high school and college credit. I accepted this opportunity and began at Pasco-Hernando Community College when I was 14 years old. At this moment you may be thinking that this was an ambitious choice for someone who could not even read at her grade level. There were two considerations for why I made this choice. One, I always felt smart. When I was able to grasp the information I could do wonderful things with it. As long as I could read what I needed to and didn't have to tell anybody that I had severe difficulties doing so, I felt that I could take on the world. Two, my parents had an enormous amount of faith in me and were essentially, from my view, un-fazed by my reading limitations.

In community college, I did have to read things that were more difficult than I had ever read before. However, for the most part I didn't have to read. Although you should always read your textbooks, I did not. I listened, asked questions, and tried to reason things out myself. I was able to get through this way without burdening myself with too many arduous reading assignments. I struggled with writing assignments, specifically with spelling and grammar. I would write up my assignments to the best of my ability and then hand them to my dad. He did not change the content ever, but he showed me my grammar errors and coached me to improve my convoluted sentences. With my dad's help I was able to flourish as a writer without being humiliated and debilitated by my writing difficulties.

I graduated with my A.A. and high school diploma when I was 16. I immediately went to the University of South Florida. At the age of 17 I was taking 3000 level classes. I realized my first semester that university professors would expect me to do a lot more reading and writing.

I remember I had to do an assignment based on a 50-page reading. I had procrastinated most of it until the last day. With the assignment due in just hours, I had to complete the reading and the written discussion post. I remember reading a paragraph and not knowing what it said and having to reread it. It was so hard to read that I got to the point that evening where I stopped after every paragraph to pray that I would have the strength to continue for just another paragraph and called my parents at least three times to get encouragement. By the time I had finished the reading I was so worn out by tears, frustration, and mental exhaustion that I certainly did not write my best discussion post. I can honestly say that was the worst reading experience of my life. After that, I knew I needed help. I started having my dad read me assignments or I would find a free audiobook copy on the Internet. Since I was at the dorm and not at home my dad rarely got to read to me and there was a great lack of audiobook availability to me at the time, so I could only use this audio support for 5% of my reading needs. I constantly had to just read, and with that I got bad headaches and felt such debilitating mental exhaustion. To read just a 50 page school assignment took me nine hours. I had to not just read but also take detailed notes so that I could protect myself from the "Swiss cheese effect."

With writing assignments I used much the same technique I did in community college. I wrote my best and then my dad edited my work. However, as I entered more difficult classes I started to get comments about my writing. I needed to be more to the point and less convoluted. Although the comments were written gently, I knew how hard it would be to change the way I write to be what they wanted it to be. I got to the point where I had to do three rewrites before I submitted something and then up to three rewrites based on the comments I received from the teacher. By the end of an assignment, I might have done up to six drafts, but the professor would only have seen two of them.

Despite my limitations, I used my strengths to succeed as best I could. I listened well. I reasoned constantly. I just tried very hard. Due to the effort I put into school, I was able to graduate Summa cum Laude and with Honors College distinction with a B.A. at the age of 19. I didn't fail classes at any point, but I did overcompensate to the point of hurting myself.

It was not until after I graduated that my reading life began to improve. When I was 18 someone had mentioned to me that I might have Dyslexia. That was the first time ever someone had suggested that. All the reasons that people before had attributed to my reading difficulties were valid, but now I had a potential diagnosis. Soon after learning about Dyslexia, I heard about Learning Ally. I was able to get a membership as a physically-disabled person. I used some of those books and increased my audio-supported reading to 15% for my last year of school. In researching Dyslexia, though, I found out I had already been compensating somewhat. I read out loud or used an audiobook when I could. There were many other things, little things, I discovered I had already been doing to help me succeed despite my Dyslexia. After graduating, I was encouraged to get a formal evaluation by a psychologist. Since doing so I have officially been diagnosed with Dyslexia.

My whole life I have been extremely ashamed of my reading difficulties. I told no one about it. Since learning about Dyslexia and the many individuals that have it, my perspective has changed. I know there are legitimate reasons why I struggle to read and write. I have found many new ways to cope better with my Dyslexia, most especially the use of text-to-speech, a computerized synthetic voice to read things to myself. I know that I can succeed despite my limitations. Although I cannot go back and be open about my reading struggles to my friends and undergraduate professors, I can now share my story. I want to stress that the second I accepted myself as a dyslexic was the second the burden of my "illiteracy" was lifted. Moreover, I am so happy to share the "tricks" I figured out that helped me succeed in college. I don't want anyone to struggle to read college material like I did, nor feel the shame I felt. With this book you will not experience what I had to, but rather have the confidence and accommodations necessary to be the best college student you can be!

CHAPTER 4 - College

Getting into College

Getting ready to look into different colleges and even apply to one is a very exciting time. Reviewing the colleges' websites is the best way to start this process. When you open that webpage you will see "Admissions" and "Academics." These two headers will lead you into the channels necessary to learn everything you need to about the school. You will want to learn about the majors offered, application requirements, tuition and financial aid, services for students with disabilities, and student life (through student organization lists, videos, and photos).

Your college inquiries are not localized to just online, though. You ought to visit the school itself. Take a guided tour of campus, visit a class, and talk to current students. Information on tours can be found on the college's website.

For the purposes of this book, having a firm understanding of the services offered to students with disabilities is vital. Those services are very important for your success at college. For example, you can receive more time on tests, use of a computer for a test, extended deadlines for term papers, textbooks converted into e-textbooks, and assistance with note taking. I, Jim, often used extra time on tests and extended deadlines for term papers. I regularly scanned, though, my own books to turn them into e-textbooks. I, Maria, took computerized tests. I was even able to use a special keyboard. I was also given a typist if I needed one, due to my own physical difficulties. One accommodation not often highlighted is the tranquility of the testing room itself. When you take a test at the Office for Students with Disabilities (SDS or SSD), you are in a quiet room on your own — no students or test-prompters bearing down on you and taking your focus away. You can talk out loud to yourself and stay focused because of the nice testing conditions SSD offers.

ACT and SAT

Many but not all four-year colleges require applicants to take the SAT or ACT when applying. In fact, there are a surprising number of colleges and universities that do not require either of these tests; for example, almost no community colleges have this requirement. The SAT and ACT evaluate your skills in reading, writing, and mathematics. They are not wholly knowledge-based, but rather are reasoning tests aimed at discerning your logic skills. Research these tests thoroughly. Choose the one right for you because you do not have to take both. When you study for the test, focus on thinking about what they are asking rather than just "computing" an answer. Learn the test, not just the answers!

You can get accommodations for your Dyslexia (or physical disability), when you take the SAT or ACT. Accommodations include extra time, a computer for writing your essay, and/or a reader to read you the test. I, Jim, took the SAT without accommodations. I scored in the 3rd percentile, which means that 97% of those taking the test scored better than I did. Fortunately, I was accepted and went to the college of my choice. When I applied to graduate school I took the Graduate Record Exam (GRE) Advanced Subject Test for Psychology with accommodations. On that test I scored in the 97th percentile, a complete reversal of my previous test results!

I, Maria, took the SAT and ACT numerous times. I went through the ACT with particular intensity, though. I completed 5 practice tests and 4 in-class tests. I knew early on that I needed to get a score of 28 to get in the Honors College at my university. The best score I ever got was a 24. However, I had increased from a 17 to a 24 with practice and using accommodations (on the first test I had no accommodations). I ended up still getting into the Honors College because I contacted the Dean and really stressed to him that I was more than a test score. I showed him that I could succeed in the Honors College and that was ultimately enough for him. I am glad that I fought to get the best score I could, but I am more glad to know that I could use my other strengths and achievements to make me desirable and more than a test score! I cannot promise that this is how it will work out for you, but know that we both did not score perfectly on a standardized test, yet still got into college and succeeded!

We recommend that you take these tests with accommodations. You should seek out accommodations for the SAT and ACT (and GRE) very early, since they all have long waiting periods before you learn if you are accepted for the accommodations of your choice. The plan to take the test in your junior year, but work to obtain accommodations in the spring of your sophomore year is not unusual. You apply for testing accommodations through your school counselor. Your counselor will need to submit documentation about your disability. This documentation includes the testing and evaluations that you did when you got approval for your IEP or 504 Plan at school. It is important that either your IEP or 504 Plan stipulate the accommodations that you need for tests. It is unlikely that the SAT or ACT will grant accommodations that you are not receiving at school. So for example, you should be receiving extra time for tests, a reader to read your tests to you or a computer to write your essays at school in order to receive these accommodations for the College Board Tests. If you are homeschooled, than you will submit the documentation yourself. Contact the SAT and ACT to learn everything about how to go about this.

Services for Students with Disabilities

If you were classified as Learning Disabled or dyslexic in high school, you may be reluctant to do so in college. You may feel that now that you have graduated from high school, it is time to leave "special education" behind. We can certainly sympathize with these feelings. Believe us when we say that as you move to college your special education experience will fade into the past. You will find that using services provided by the Office for Students with Disabilities (SDS or SSD) differs greatly from your high school experience. Additionally, you need to keep in mind that your main goal is getting through college successfully to acquire your degree.

The helpfulness of SSD varies greatly from college to college. Some SSD programs excel in scanning books for students and say they will help students learn to scan their own textbooks. Before making a final decision about a college make sure you are happy with their SSD!

In order to access SSD you will have to apply to their office. This requires submitting documentation of your disability. Documentation for Dyslexia (a learning disability) usually includes an evaluation report from a psychologist trained in educational evaluations. The report must include the results of an intelligence test and the results from achievement (reading) tests. You can have these tests done while you are in high school by your district's school psychologist. This testing must be done at the age of 16 or older. These tests can be done as part of your transition plan from high school to college. We recommend that you have this done in your junior year of high school. If your district cannot do this testing, you will need to arrange for psycho-educational testing. Be sure, if you contact a psychologist for your evaluation, that he is trained in and will conduct psycho-educational testing to verify your Dyslexia.

When you apply to the SSD Office, you will have to indicate the types of accommodations that you will need. Your SSD counselor will help you do this. The most common accommodations include help with scanning textbooks, extra time on tests, extra time to complete term papers, a computer for taking tests, and/or a reader to read test questions to you. After this application process, the SSD Office will give you a letter to give to each of your professors at the beginning of the semester explaining the accommodations you are entitled to for your class.

Once you have this letter you are guaranteed these accommodations. Note that it will be up to you to meet with your professor to arrange accommodations and he is never privy to what your actual disability is. These represent a major departure from high school policy. You will be expected to act more independently in arranging your accommodations. Again, it varies greatly with colleges how involved your SSD Office will be in assisting you. However, you will definitely be expected to be your own advocate. For example, if you have testing accommodations, you will be expected to call the university testing center (or go online) to arrange the date and time for your class tests.

We strongly encourage you to use the college's services for students with disabilities. We both used these services. Believe us, the academic challenges of college are rigorous, but having accommodations levels the playing field for you. You should make sure that you are not placed at a disadvantage by your Dyslexia!

Community College

If you are not sure whether or not you are ready for a four-year college, then community college is a great stepping stone. We both have gone to community college — Jim as a traditional young college student and Maria as a dual-enrolled high school student. Community college is a great experience! Fortunately, tuition and costs at a community college are less than a four-year college. Thus, you will pay or borrow less to receive a high-quality college education. The less money you owe or have to pay to receive an education, the easier it will be when you get out of college.

Community colleges' small class size provide the best advantage to students. Most introductory classes have 25-30 students, whereas typical introductory classes at large universities have 150-300 students. Jim's music classes at community college usually only had 10 or fewer students. Most likely you will have a good opportunity to get to know your professors and to ask questions, because professors at community college are more available than at the large universities. Although class difficulty can be comparable to a University classroom, often the classes are toned down in their intensity, have lighter expectations on the student, and are more focused on individual student success. Thus, community college is a great middle step before university.

Large University Versus Small College
When you do go to four-year college, take into consideration its size. I, Jim, have attended both small (5,000 students) and large (40,000 students) colleges. Again there was a big difference in class size! At my smaller college, I rarely had a class bigger than 15, but at

my large college many classes had 50 or more students (except for advanced classes which had around 25). I got to know my professors really well at the small college. However, at the large university, professors were unavailable due to the immense class size. There, I had to talk with graduate teaching assistants (called T.A.'s) to get my questions answered. On the other hand, large universities have the advantage of offering more diverse classes. Therefore, you can easily find classes that interest you. Also these universities offer a better extracurricular experience. Further, undergraduates have an opportunity to participate in research and experimentation with professors or graduate students, something I, Maria, did and very much enjoyed. Though I went to a large university, I was part of a small department. This helped me experience all the advantages of small class size and available professors akin to a small college, but still have the resources of my large institution. If you plan to go to graduate school after college there is usually no particular advantage to the size of the college you have attended.

CHAPTER 5 - Tackling the Reading Challenge

Reading and writing are perhaps the two most used skills in college. While in high school, you could count on your teacher reviewing much of your textbook in class. In college, even though the professors lecture, much of what they talk about will be in addition to material in the textbook. The amount of reading you do differs greatly depending on the major field you study. Majors like mathematics and chemistry require less reading than majors like history or English. For most majors we estimate that you will spend over half of your study time reading.

By the second week of college I, Jim, figured that I needed my books read to me in order to keep up with assignments. On my own I read 40 words per minute (wpm) which came to about 5 or 6 textbook pages in an hour. Typical class assignments were to read 20 to 25 pages. So every week in a class I was expected to read 60 or more pages per subject. All the way through undergraduate and graduate school all of my textbooks were either audio files from Learning Ally, digitized books from Bookshare or digitized books which I created by scanning the print textbook. Even today it is impossible for me to read books unless they are digitized and read to me. This type of reading we call audio-supported reading. With audio-supported reading I can read 180-200 wpm, equaling 20 textbook pages an hour. Some people like to read with very rapid text-to-speech rates of 300-400 wpm. I do not like such high speeds, but reading rate is a very individual preference.

Jim's Highlighting Method

Here is a description of Jim's method for reading textbooks and highlighting. During my freshman year I would read an assignment once and highlight the important points in my textbook. When studying for tests I would read my highlights and class notes to myself. This generally netted me a C and at worst a D. Mind you, I would read over these notes and highlights several times. If I read them only once it definitely was a D. In order to ensure myself a C, I would read over and test myself several times during the week heading to the in-class test.

After several years I decided on psychology as a major. I knew that I wanted to go to graduate school to become a psychologist. I talked with my friend Dave who was also prepping to become a psychologist. He assured me that one needed mostly A's to get into graduate school. He was right. So I changed my tactics for reading and studying. I now read (listened to) my assigned chapters twice on two different days. This gave me a much better understanding of the chapters being assigned. I also held off highlighting important points until the second reading. This strategy really paid off. I made many fewer highlights, which helped me to focus upon the really important ideas. Additionally, I asked some fellow students to read my highlights and class notes to me. As they read I recorded them. In this way my rereading was much more effective than my own reading. Nowadays, one can have the computer do this extra reading. I acquired Kurzweil 3000 (K3000) software. With this software I scanned my books and read them on the computer. One of the advantages of K3000 is that it not only allows for highlighting important points but you can focus and read just the highlights back to yourself. This approach netted me mostly B's.

Then I developed my formula for getting straight A's. I often used K3000. Now most of my reading and studying is done using books from Bookshare or scanned books and reading using *Voice Dream Reader* on my iPad. Instead of reading text twice, I read text three times. I will read a chapter once making no highlights or notes. This gives me a solid "lay of the land" of the material. I also do this reading prior to class to reduce my need for note taking. Then a few days later, I read the chapter a second time. This time I mark important points. I only mark key words and highlight significant sentences. While getting ready for tests I will read my highlights a number of times. For example, within *Voice Dream Reader* you scroll through the book. When a highlight is encountered you double tap with one finger on the first word of the highlight which starts the reading. A double tap with two fingers stops the reading. Then the day before the test I read the complete chapters for a third time non-stop. This final reading is miraculous, since it has the effect of incorporating the reading into my mind as if I were the actual author of the text. This always gets me A's and solid knowledge.

Maria's Highlighting Method

As you read — whether with an audiobook, text-to-speech, or just yourself — you can add different types of notes to the text itself. Hand written/typed notes can be attached to a certain passage or word. A bookmark can be enjoined to a page. Lastly, colored highlights can be imposed on specially selected text with either a real highlighter or one built-in to a reading app. All of the notes can be accessed in the "Notes" tab on the book options menu (for an app) or on the page itself. Whether you take notes in a physical book, in a notebook, or on a screen, there are ways to do it that help you grasp the text better.

Since I have difficulty reading, it is critical that I make the most out of my reading experience. I do not want to finish reading and have no clue what I just read. I do not want to struggle to find things again within the text. Even though being read to dramatically improves my ability to read, I still need to work hard to truly understand and remember what I read. To accomplish this, I employ annotations — like highlights and notes — to help me keep track of important sentences and actively engage with the text itself while I read.

I went to school to study history and fine arts, so my perspective on reading is different from Jim's. I read a lot of primary sources — i.e. works written in the past, such as the eighth-century *Life of Saint Cuthbert* by Bede. I also read academic books, where authors discuss primary sources and argue their opinions about those sources using their collected evidence; these are called secondary sources. As I suggest ways to actively engage with your reading, I will separate my comments between those dedicated to primary sources and those to secondary sources. Learning the difference between these types of sources and how best to analyze them is something for your own coursework. Here I want to merely offer ways to take beneficial notes while reading, so as to help you actively read them.

Primary Sources

While taking humanities courses, I devised a method to read literary works and take notes at the same time. Before beginning reading, I would ask myself what the reading was to be used for. Would I use it to talk about women, politics, or miracles — just to name a few? Answering this helps narrow down my focus when I read. I then thought of important points or categories for the topic of the week; I made a list of them. As an example, for "women" I listed points such as motherhood and femininity. As I read the material, I made notes beside certain sections that I felt exemplified one or more of the categories I had made ahead of time. Thus, I wrote "motherhood" beside a quote that specifically mentioned a mother or was by a mother. When I looked back on the text to find quotes or excerpts, I only needed to look at the keywords I had written in the margins rather than trying to find something in the dense text. This also works if you use an app or Kindle to take notes. In the "notes" list you will see your typed notes; simply tap that and you will be directed to that specific excerpt. Planning ahead to what you will note makes a big difference when you go back through trying to find something. Certainly, comment on observations and ideas as well, but I am always partial to an incisive keyword.

Color highlights, another way to mark your book, stand out on the page and help you connect with the selected excerpt. I use color highlighters all the time when I read on my Kindle. Kindle offers four colors: yellow, blue, red, and orange. Please, determine what each color will signify before you start reading and using the highlighters. I will tell you how I use these four colors for literary works, but know that decision is ultimately your very own.

Yellow - Passages significant to the story line, e.g. character development, significant events, etc.
Blue - Historical facts or context, e.g. reference to real historical practices, books, etc.
Red - Passages vital to remember
Orange - Scintillating quotations applicable either to life or a school assignment

Secondary Sources

I did not have to read many textbooks in college, a perk of being a humanities major. My secondary reading centered around scholarly books and articles. The intensity of these readings varied greatly, but they had a uniform purpose. The authors put forth an argument and defend it. The argument stands out in a clear thesis statement. Moreover, often each section or paragraph has an intention sentence to guide the reader. As a reader you must follow the author and actively engage with the argument and evidence. I still write/type out an outline to help me best follow the author. If I rewrite it, then I must work hard to understand it. If I use an eReader then I employ color highlights to follow the text. Here is a color breakdown again:

Yellow - Passages that add to the whole, such as evidence or author's opinions.

Blue - Anything slightly outside the author's argument that needs to be remembered, e.g. historical context. I may also use this color to highlight other secondary sources referenced by the author that I want to look up later.

Red - Passages vital to remember

Orange - Thesis statements and section/paragraph intention sentences

Secondary sources are difficult to read. Practice and good instruction from professors can improve your ability. As you begin to better understand how to read secondary material then employing note stratagems will further cement your understanding and will help you review the material. Holding on to that moment when you best understand what you read remains the goal whenever you use annotations.

A Note on Extra Reading

As I, Jim, was in graduate school I discovered the value of doing extra reading. There were the usual textbooks and research papers to do the reading for, but I also read some additional outside reading. I even did outside reading in statistics. What kind of outside reading did I do? I searched for books that provided extra explanations to my courses. For example, I took courses in statistics. My outside readings were books that often explained the nature of statistical techniques in verbal descriptions instead of mathematical formulas. Or when I took a course on personality, I read a reference book which gave very good summaries of the different theories of personality. Additionally, I found when taking courses it was helpful to use easy-to-read foundational material on the subject. Often this foundation could be found in the series of books called "The Complete Idiot's Guide To..." or the "...For Dummies" series. I've read such books as Anatomy & Physiology For Dummies or Complete Idiot's

Guide to American History. These titles leave something to be desired, but the content is great. I have used books from these series frequently while tutoring students. These easy-to-read books often give an extra look at important principles and facts in a field of study, while the class textbooks were often drowning in too many details. I frequently got more from these extra books then from the books assigned in class.

Your College Library

You will most likely read some books from your college library. At this library a wide assortment of books are in ready supply. Libraries are organized by categories. Reference material — such as encyclopedias and dictionaries — normally are housed in one spot, but in the humanities, literature and non-fiction books will be intermingled among each other. In the sciences and social sciences, books on a particular subject area will be collected together on the same or nearby shelves. The easiest way to find a book is to search for it in the online catalogue — these days only a few taps on your smartphone will bring it up for you. Often when you look up a book that you are interested in, going to the library bookshelves can be very handy. You might ask how best to read these print copies of books? In other sections of our book we discuss the process of scanning books to create your own digital ebooks.

Your professors may often have particular books or parts of books that they want you to read. This is referred to as assigned reading. Often these assigned readings are kept at a particular checkout desk. You are allowed to checkout the book or article for a few hours at a time. It would be helpful to make a copy of the assigned chapter or article that you can scan to your computer in order to have it read to you.

Physical Books

The world is far from short of tangible books. From your local library to your University library, these books line thousands of shelves, eager to be embraced and perused. Libraries are organized by category. The easiest way to find a book is to search for it in the online catalogue. Keep in mind, due to this categorical system of organization, like books are clustered together. If you go to a shelf in search of one book you may find two or three others of equal value in the surrounding area. Those other books may not always show up in your search because your keywords may not have warranted their appearance in your results list. Remember this when considering ways to find books to read; a trip to the library itself may be just as valuable as one to the online catalogue!

Textbooks

Almost every class you take will have a textbook assigned with the class. A big difference between high school and college is that you will actually be expected to read your assigned textbook. Often these textbooks are over 800-1,000 pages in length. Such textbooks in high school lasted you the entire year. But in college such books are used for a single semester's work. So you can see your reading is piling up fast. Since you own the print book or have it in electronic format, you can mark it up all you like. In fact highlighting and marking important material will be a key strategy in your reading and studying. Most students buy highlighters of different colors to mark important facts in their reading, and often e-textbooks have digital highlighters to do the same.

Ebooks

Coursework will require that you retain certain books for the remainder of the semester. Your research for a course may require you to read whole books. Not to mention, you may want to personally enrich yourself with books. Certainly a library full of print books will provide the reading material necessary for any venture, but as dyslexics, we need to put in a lot of elbow-grease to read print books. Since some books may not be available as audiobooks, we may need to scan them to have them read to us. Thus, buying or renting an ebook (electronic book) provides a compelling solution; through the wonder of technology you can read any amount of pages in an ebook at any time without having to scan the book yourself. Today there are many ebook venders, but how do you navigate the options? Certainly, where you buy your books is up to you, but this short overview may help you.

iBooks, Kindle, Nook, and Google Play Books are the major ebook vendors. They have mobile and desktop apps. The most popular books may cost over $10, but there are many books for under $5. Of course, public-domain books, books published before 1923, are free. Purchased books are stored in the respective app and in the respective cloud. Kindle and Nook sell textbooks as well as reading books. Often they offer a rent option so you can keep the book for the whole semester at a reduced price.

If you do not want to buy an ebook, whether due to expense or not, then consider using *OverDrive*. This is a brilliant service that connects you with your local public library's digital collections online, as long as you have a library card. Moreover, you can borrow audiobooks and ebooks from your library to have on your mobile device. Having access to free professional audiobooks is especially beneficial and nice. Ebooks often can even be sent to your Kindle bookshelf itself during your lending period, where you can read them like any other Kindle ebook. Your public library probably has more popular ebooks than academic ones.

Your college library will also have ebooks in their catalogue. Sadly, we do not know of any way to get these ebooks to appear on your mobile device or eReader. They can be accessed on a web browser through your university online catalogue. I, Maria, have collected a list of different types of ebooks used by colleges, employing my University as a resource; thus, my list may differ somewhat from that of your own University. Principally, there are four different ebook platforms:

EBL (part of the Ebook Corporation)

ACLS Humanities Ebooks (part of the Michigan Library System)

Cambridge Series / Springer Link / JSTOR

Your university's own format

Some will show the ebook within a special window; others will have you download PDFs of individual chapters. Further down I explain how to make each of these formats capable of being read with text-to-speech on a computer or mobile device. The process to check out these ebooks may differ from regular books. Policies about ebooks differ from library to library. Here is an example of my university's policy: you can "check out" one book for 24-hours or three days. You may access this book as many times and for as long as you want during this lending period. That means that this title is then unavailable for others to read during this lending period. If you ever cannot open an ebook within your library online catalogue, it may be because someone else is reading that title. Formats aside, university libraries can provide you with ebooks that are either too hard to get or too expensive to own. It is truly a wonderful resource!

All the above ebook resources can be accessed and used by all college students and even most lay people. As someone with a print disability, though, you have an additional resource for ebooks: Bookshare! Bookshare supplies over 307,000 ebooks to print-impaired readers. You must have a diagnosed print disability — like Dyslexia — to use this special online library. You can download the books to your computer or there are several mobile apps to read Bookshare ebooks, each discussed later. All the apps display the text of the book and highlight the text as it is read aloud. Bookshare has many popular and classic books. We can also attest they have a fair academic book section, complete with several Cambridge Companions. When searching for ebooks, Bookshare should be one of your first stops.

A note of caution: navigation of these ebooks is quite unlike a physical book. True, the table of contents will direct you to the chapters and a separate annotations breakdown will show you all your highlights, but you can only see one page at a time and you cannot flip through the pages quickly. The text appearance itself is very editable; you can change the font type and size, but remember the larger you make the font the more pages you have to turn to complete a traditional paper page. Our point here is that ebooks take some adjustment. It takes time to get used to the navigation and the appearance of ebooks as well as just reading on a screen all the time. We are here to say that it can be done with great, great success! With dedication the eccentricities of ebooks will pass away and the full advantages of independent reading can be enjoyed. I, Maria, have come to prefer to read an ebook over a tangible book. When I read tangible books before, I had to hold the book close to my eyes to stay focused on the text and not get lost with all those words. With an ebook I just make the font large enough without having to hold the device too close to myself. Even my annotations are better on an ebook. Before, I would write marginal notes that I could not read later, but on an ebook I can type out my notes ensuring that I can read them later (note: Kindle enables you to export your ebook annotations through their website kindle.amazon.com). Ebooks offer you such independence; it is worth the adjustment!

Journal Articles

I, Jim, will write about reading journal articles in the social sciences. Journal articles in the social sciences, as well as the "hard" sciences, are essentially write ups of experiments done by research scientists or science teams. The format for social sciences is quite standardized. The sections of an article are as follows: abstract about the research, introduction giving a short literature review of the research area under discussion, description of the subjects in the research, research methodology or how the experiment was conducted, results of the research and a discussion and summary of the research and findings.

When you do a research paper in the social sciences, you read a number of research articles, say 10 or 15, and you review the findings of the research. Often, you may be asked to propose what you might do if you were a researcher in the field of study. Hence you write up your paper in the form of an experiment with an introduction to the research topic, discussion of your hypothesis to research, description of the research methodology for conducting the experiment and a description of the statistical techniques you would use to analyze you data. After this write up, you would be in the position to do the research. Often in social science laboratory classes you actually do run the research you have proposed. In those cases, you write up your experimental findings and end with a discussion of the significance of your results. If your research was unique enough, you could actually submit your research for publication in a journal. I've known several undergraduates who did just that. When I was in graduate school, I published several of my experiments.

Making Books Accessible

With all the books you will need to read in college, you may not have control over the format of each and every one. No matter what book you need to read there is a way to make it accessible to you. Here follows an overview of different scenarios you may find yourself in and methods to make that reading material accessible.

I have a physical book I bought or received from the library

We are happy to report there are multiple options in this situation. You can search for the audio book on Learning Alley and digital book on Bookshare to see if it is already in an accessible format. You can see if there is an ebook version available for purchase or rent through vendors and libraries listed above. Admittedly, many scholarly books are not popular enough to be available through these avenues. In that case, you can take the book and scan it, either at your college library or at home; please see the "scanning" section for a full description of this option. Regardless of the book, with a little effort you can find a way to have it read to you.

I have an eBook

With an iDevice you can easily read ebooks. VoiceOver supports reading ebooks from iBooks, Kindle, Google Play, and Nook ebooks. With VoiceOver turned on, stroke with a two-finger swipe down to start the reading. You can start on whatever page you would like and stop at anytime with a two-finger tap of the screen. More about this below.

I have a Kindle and Kindle eBooks

Kindles come with a high-quality text-to-speech voice built-in. With text-to-speech on, you can turn the speech on and off by tapping the play button found at the bottom right of the book menu. See the "Kindle" section for a fuller explanation.

I have a College Library eBook

We listed the different ebook formats above. The process to have them read to you can be quite complex or easy. Here follows a breakdown for each different format:

EBL (part of the Ebook Corporation) EBL provides academic ebooks to university libraries. There are over 500,000 ebooks in all kinds of subject areas. All titles have a read-aloud feature.

Option A) Use the built-in reader. Select "Read" on the top menu within the book itself. You cannot change the speed rate.

Option B) Click "download" on the top menu. That will send a copy of the book for 24 hours to *Adobe Digital Edition*, which is a computer application akin to Kindle and iBook. With *Adobe Digital Edition*, you can use your computer's text-to-speech to read the book and you can also adjust the font size.

Option C) Select the "Print" feature to make a PDF of a selected chapter. Then you can send that to whatever app you would like to have it read to you.

ACLS Humanities Ebooks (part of the Michigan Library System) The ACLS is a collection of 4,300 books that are important to the Humanities. These are books that are frequently required for reading and research.

Option A) You have the choice to view the page as an image, text, or PDF. Choose the "text" option and then simply use the text-to-speech on your computer to read the text.

Option B) After you select the chapter your want to read with the table of contents, view the page as a PDF (note: it will clump several pages into one PDF). Download as many groups of pages as you need until you know you have covered the chapter. You can now use those PDFs to read the chapter, but you must manually combine them to create the whole chapter PDF and manually digitize the text with an OCR software.

Cambridge Series / Springer Link / JSTOR

Option A) All three of these services work the same way. They have you download chapters of their books as a PDF. As a PDF you can then take it to whatever place you want in order to get it read to you. The PDF will most likely be locked.

All other ebook formats

Option A) Use the "Print" feature to make a PDF of a selected chapter. Then you can send that to whatever app you would like. The PDFs undoubtedly will be locked. Quick tip: You will be restricted on how many pages "to print." If you cannot get enough of the book exported as a

PDF for what you need to do, then ask your friends to help you export some more of the text on their own accounts.

Working with PDFs

A Portable Document Format (PDF) is a file that looks just like a printed page, only it remains on your computer or mobile device. It cannot be edited, but rather holds on to the final document customizations that were made before it was transformed into a PDF. PDFs are extremely handy because they can be read on many platforms without changing format. Today, they are used readily in a variety of different ways.

Journal Articles

Journal articles are essays written by scholars, thematically collected together on a regular basis and bound in scholarly journals (akin to anthologies). Journals are printed, but today they are also published electronically. Articles within journals can be accessed individually, both through the publisher and through databases. Databases are storehouses for bibliographic citations, journal articles, newspaper articles, and/or pictures. You can access databases through your college library online catalogue. In the database you search with keywords, and articles, among other things, will come up in the results list. Most often you will download journal articles as PDFs.

These PDFs vary widely in quality. Some PDFs may have been digitized post-publication of the article and therefore do not have "smart-text" — digitally readable text under the text image. Others may have smart-text, but in reality they are quite "dumb" indeed. For these articles you could see text like this, "Here I argue," but under that, the digitally readable text will say, "hereiargue." Still others may be published electronically simultaneously with the print edition and therefore be perfect smart-text, the over and under text matching up exactly. This is due to the PDF having been rendered directly from some type of word processor rather than scanned from a paper document. This difference in quality will have great significance in making the PDF text-to-speech accessible. Also, these PDFs are always "complex texts." They will have headers and footers, footnotes/endnotes, often tables, and maybe even be structured in two-column format.

Book Chapters

Above we noted several times that book chapters can be saved as PDFs. You will either download them this way from a publisher — such as Cambridge Press — or form them when you scan a book. They operate much the same as any other PDF, just keep in mind that the PDF page is exactly like the printed book page.

Handmade PDFs

If a PDF is not made by a publisher then it would be considered a handmade PDF. You can make PDFs on most word processors —including *Word* and *Pages* — by "exporting [your document] as" PDF. If you "print" a web page, often you can choose to "save as" PDF instead, which serves as another way to create a PDF. Lastly, some software may have you export information as a PDF — such as the OpticBook scanner.

In your college classes you will be given many handouts, like the class syllabus. Often the teachers will publish that handout as a PDF online as well. Nearly always, these PDFs are made from an editable document so the PDF will have accurate smart-text. Handmade PDFs can be the best PDFs because they are either already at a fantastic quality or you can control the circumstances to make them high-quality.

Sometimes you may need to combine several PDFs to make a single larger, complete PDF. This is especially true if you want to cobble together scanned PDF pages to make a book chapter. The techniques vary greatly to do this, so please consult Youtube videos to find how to do it on your PDF preview software. We are not aware of methods to combine PDF pages from different PDFs on a mobile device.

Making PDFs Accessible

PDFs are quite different from ebooks and word documents in one specific respect, they do not make a distinction between the table of contents, body text, footnotes, etc. Although PDFs look structured and organized, below that image is just straight text. Using text-to-speech puts a spotlight on this fact. When a synthetic voice reads a PDF as is, it cannot skip page numbers, headers, and footnotes because it cannot tell the difference between that and just the body text. When you read a PDF yourself you can naturally know to make the distinction, but the synthetic voice cannot, due to the way PDFs are internally formatted. Another consideration when reading a PDF is whether it is locked or not. To lock a PDF means to prevent anyone from changing the PDF in any way. This means you cannot rescan the PDF or even save your highlights. If a PDF comes from a publisher— ebook chapters especially — it is often locked. Journal articles and handmade PDFs are more often than not unlocked. These are the things that we need to ponder when we go to have a PDF read to us. So, our discussion is split between locked and unlocked PDFs, with unlocked PDFs further split into non-smart-text and smart-text PDFs.

Locked PDFs

Sadly, there is not much you can do if the PDF is locked. Luckily, locked PDFs tend to have excellent smart-text. The best solution, therefore, is to highlight and select only a portion of the text, such as a paragraph, to be read rather than having everything read in one fluid motion. Most of the software we discuss, which reads PDFs, can do this. This way you can bypass all the headers and footnotes when you read the body text.

Unlocked PDFs

The difficulty in reading unlocked PDFs varies greatly based on the quality of the PDFs. An unlocked PDF that is simple, without headers and footnotes, and with excellent smart-text needs essentially nothing. Just open the PDF on your computer or mobile device with a program that can read PDFs and read! An unlocked PDF that is complex, even with great smart-text, may require more steps if you do not want to just read it by selection. You treat the PDF much like you would one that is completely without smart-text. Here are instructions for what I, Maria, do to read PDFs, whether they originally had smart-text or not: First, analyze the PDF with *FineReader Pro* (an OCR software). Then, go back through the PDF and unhighlight/deselect all page numbers, headers, in-page footnotes, and picture captions. During this process also make sure it analyzed the text correctly. It may think a shadow is an extra word or a picture. Either delete or re-adjust the text box. If you re-adjust anything, right-click the box and "analyze the object" to ensure your change will stick. After you have edited the analyzation, click "read" again to cement all your changes.

At this point, export the file as either a PDF, EPUB, or Word document. I like to export the file twice, once as a PDF and another as an EPUB. I export as a PDF because I always want the original, where the most accurate text and format is, to be close at hand. I also like to have the EPUB because the file is smaller than the PDF. With an EPUB or Word document version I can have the synthetic voice serve as an audiobook narrator, with specific software, and I can view the original PDF on a non-assistive application. On the other hand, I can choose to read the PDF as an EPUB on a mobile device or Kindle just like any other ebook. The goal is to make the PDF as easy to understand as possible when it is being read. Sometimes a little extra work can provide a better experience and is hence worth it.

Tips for Optimal Reading of PDFs

Admittedly, reading PDFs is almost identical to reading books in terms of understanding and skills. We cannot offer different advice, but instead refer you to the section above where we discuss reading books. This is true with one exception. Before you start reading a PDF, decide where you will store your annotations; keep them in one place. If you read half a Journal article as a PDF on your computer, but then finish it on your Kindle, the highlights and notes will not necessarily magically sync.

If you read a handout as a EPUB, your PDF version will not have any of the annotations you make. I, Maria, have made this mistake so many times where I have notes in three different places. There are two solutions to this. One, decide where you will read the PDF (as either a PDF or EPUB) and stick with that. Two, keep some notes in a notebook or Word document. Separate notes ensure you have everything in one place no matter where you read the PDF.

CHAPTER 6 - Tips for Supporting Your Reading

Getting and Reading Books from Bookshare

Bookshare Books

Bookshare is a library for print-impaired readers. Not all Bookshare books are academic in nature, and many are for entertainment. Like your public library, Bookshare makes ebooks available to be checked out. You must have a diagnosis of a print disability, like dyslexia, to use this special online library. Bookshare has over 317,000 e-books in their collection. While in college you can request Bookshare to scan a book for you and give you an ebook of it. Two iPad/iPhone apps can be used to read Bookshare e-books. These are *Voice Dream Reader* and *Read2Go*. On Android devices you can use the *GoRead* and *Darwin Reader* apps. Each app displays the text of the book and highlights the text as it is read aloud. The reading voices for these apps are quite good. Each app has the ability to look up and download books from Bookshare.

Voice Dream Reader [iOS]

Voice Dream Reader reads imported Word, Text, Web, Bookshare, and EPUB documents. It is our first choice for reading Bookshare books on an Apple mobile device, and Maria's very favorite iOS text reader! Significantly, *Voice Dream Reader* offers the widest selection of reading voices and provides the best customization options for font styles and color and voice speed — *Voice Dream* is the only app that allows you to set voice speed by designating words per minute (WPM). The WPM gives the greatest flexibility for selecting your preferred voice speed; Voice Dream can be set from 110 to 700 WPM. I, Jim, prefer to read at 210 WPM. I, Maria, sometimes choose to read quite fast depending on the text density because it helps me stay focused.

You can choose between nine different font styles, one of which is "OpenDyslexic" font, designed specifically for dyslexic readers. Font size can be selected in increments of 1. Additionally, character spacing and line spacing can also be adjusted. Research has demonstrated that dyslexics read better when there is extra space between letters and lines. You can also select how many lines are visible while reading; you can choose between 1, 3, 5, or all the lines to be shown. We both prefer the entire screen to be filled with text. The ability to select both font and background color also supplies great help. *Voice Dream* comes with default styles but everything is changeable to meet your own desires.

Although many programs highlight the sentence and word while reading, *Voice Dream* stands out by highlighting the line and word being read. You have the option to turn on and off either word or line highlighting. We both prefer just line highlighting, since the extra word highlighting is visually too busy and hard to follow. You can bookmark important points. When reviewing bookmarks you can read them by simply doing a single finger double tap where you wish to read. Easy read-back of bookmarks is very important as a study tool.

The ability to import a wealth of different file formats really propels *Voice Dream* to true excellence. You can send your word documents to *Voice Dream* and copy in a text from a website. Bookshare and Project Gutenberg are incorporated into the app for easy download of their files, but really any EPUB can be imported. In addition to being a document reader, *Voice Dream* can read webpages two different ways. One, you can sync your *Pocket* or Instapaper account with *Voice Dream*. Two, open a webpage within the *Voice Dream* app (found under the + icon) and choose "smart save," then the body text of the article will be saved to be read at your leisure. The most excellent customization options, ease of use, and multiple file document importation for $9.99 make this app a leader among mobile text readers!

Read2Go [iOS]

Read2Go is an app designed by Bookshare for Apple mobile devices. The app comes with two high quality English voices from Acapela, one male (Ryan) and one female (Heather). You can adjust the voice speed by percent, from 60% to 260%. Font size can be changed from 10 to 70 point, though the font style is not adjustable. The app highlights both sentence and word being read. There are sixteen different colors for font background and highlighting. I, Jim, like to have a black background, yellow font, and maroon highlighting. While reading, you can bookmark important points for study or rereading. This bookmark color is also customizable. If your Bookshare book has images, *Read2Go* allows you to view them within the app. This app sells for $19.99.

GoRead [Android]

GoRead is the Bookshare Android app, though not quite as versatile or polished as the *Read2Go* app for iOS. Text, background, and highlight colors can be adjusted in the options using a red, green, and blue slider combination. Voice type and speed are controlled by the Android OS, under accessibility text-to-speech options. The main utility to this software is the ability to have a text reader on an Android phone. However, a significant issue with the app is that it always reads the top paragraph at the beginning of a page but does not then read down the page. Instead, the page keeps scrolling with the paragraph being read remaining at the top. This makes the reading awkward; though, for those who have a difficult time keeping their place on the page this structure could be a benefit.

Darwin Reader [Android]

The *Darwin Reader* app reads Bookshare books. The reading voice derives from the pre-installed voices on the Android OS, found in the accessibility setting options. The speech rate for the voice can be selected within the Darwin Reader and varies from 1 to 10 in increments of 1. I, Jim, prefer to read at speech rate 6. Admittedly, bookmarking important text is a bit awkward within the app. However, there is a healthy amount of display customization options. Font sizes vary from small to humongous. Line spacing can be set from 75% to 200%. You can select the colors for the text, highlighted text, page background, and paragraph background from a color palette within the app. Interestingly, the color options for the highlighted text being read are not the usual colors found in most apps. The text being read appears in a different color. This special colorization makes the sentence being read stand out and not be masked in any way. I set the general background to olive green and the paragraph being spoken to dark blue. The general text is in muted rose while the text being read is in vibrant yellow. I find that this customization makes the sentence being read very easy to follow. In fact, this provides such ease to my reading that the *Darwin Reader* is my favorite app for reading Bookshare books on an Android device.

Scanning books

Have you ever considered scanning your books to create ebooks? Many different resources are available to help you scan the books you own and turn them into ebooks. These resources include software within suites by *Kurzweil 3000, Read & Write Gold,* and *Premier Assistive Literacy.* Many print-impaired individuals scan some of their books in order to have the book read aloud to them. In the United States individuals with a print disability have the legal right to scan books in order to have them read aloud with a synthetic voice. Contrarily, for those without a print disability the current copyright law casts scanning books into a bit of a gray area. Scanning a book you own is often called "fair use." Moreover, in many countries individuals are allowed to scan their books as long as they retain a copy of the original print book.

Opticbook 3800 Scanner [Mac and PC]

Having the right scanner greatly contributes to producing a good scanned book. We both use an OpticBook 3800 Scanner (around $300). If you plan to scan a number of books, as we have, this scanner is a very good investment. It is built specifically for scanning books: the flatbed carries over to the very edge of the scanner. This allows you to place the book spine on the edge of the scanner rather than hurting the spine by forcing the book to lay flat. Moreover, this design enables the scanner to reach into the crease of the book, ensuring an even scan of all the text. The OpticBook 3800 has our highest recommendation. This scanner works with both Windows and Macintosh computers (note: Mac software is only at the beta level, but I, Maria, have used it with great success).

To scan a book, simply, lay the book page down on the scanner; make sure to let the rest of the book dangle so the book page will remain flat. Before scanning you can choose to make the output black and white, gray scale, or color. If you have a book page containing just text, we suggest you use black and white. If your page has a chart or graph on it, then set the machine to gray scale. For pages with colored pictures, the color output would be best. After you set the color, hit the "scan" button to scan the page of the book. The scanner will produce a PDF page for the single book page; the PDF pages will need to be grouped together separately. Scanned pages are saved in a specific folder on your computer. These images will be fairly small. A whole book file will remain suitably small. The true utility of this product lies in its brilliant efficient design, preserving the book's physical integrity and producing high-quality scans.

FineReader Pro [Mac and PC]

After you have your book scanned, you will need an Optical Character Recognition (OCR) software to digitize the words on the scanned page. OCR software takes the images of your pages and changes these images into editable text. A good OCR program will distinguish between pictures and text on a page and both the pictures and text will be saved in the output document. In our opinion, the best OCR software is ABBYY *FineReader Pro* ($169 and under. Note: you can receive a discount as a college student). FineReader automatically analyzes each page image and recognizes the text and graphics. However, you can choose to manually draw text and graphic boxes on each page image. For simple books the program analyzes the pages very well. Complex books (those with many footnotes and tables), on the other hand, may warrant manual analyzation of the pages. When you are done, you can export your file as a Word document, a PDF, or an ebook (EPUB).

I, Maria, am especially fond of *FineReader*'s expert language recognition; they offer all the modern languages and even Latin! I often set multiple languages before I analyze an academic text because inevitably scholars cite foreign articles or include foreign-language quotations.

I, Jim, frequently scan books from the library using *FineReader Pro* and then convert them into Word documents. From there I take the Word document and submit it to the Bookshare library to make the scanned book available to others. I also convert the Word document into an audio MP3 file to be listened to using my iPod Touch.

Scan and Read Pro [Mac and PC]

Scan and Read Pro does what the name implies. It is a straight forward software for scanning books and documents which then can be read aloud. Scanning is simplified. When using *Scan and Read Pro*, first, select your scanner to use with the software. Hit the "scan" button and the software will complete the scan and the OCR to generate digital text. Then, click the "read" button to have the text read, with sentence and word highlighting. Text is presented in a Word document format. The strength of this software is its ease of use and affordability. The drawback is that the resulting text from the scan does not look exactly the same as the page of the book or document. All of the text is there, just in a simple Word document format. Scan and Read Pro costs $149.95 or can be purchased as part of the Premier Literacy Productivity Pack for $245.95.

Kurzweil 3000 Professional [Mac and PC]

The all inclusive nature — scanning, reading, studying, and writing — of *Kurzweil 3000 Professional* (*K3000*) secures its place as a critical assistive tool. With such utility a sizable expense follows; it costs $1,395, but if you are enrolled in a subject major that requires lots of scanning, this may be a good option for you.

The scanning feature operates nicely. A toolbar listing each of *K3000*'s functions comes with the software. Simply, select the scanner function to begin the process. Then, select the scanner to be used and then hit the scan button itself. The ultimate scan looks exactly like the page scanned, a brilliant feature. I, Jim, particularly like the fact the pages look just like the original book and are read as if you were reading the hard copy book.

Prizmo [iOS, and in a slightly different incarnation, Mac]

Prizmo (iOS - $9.99) is a scanning, OCR, and text-to-speech app for iOS devices. To use *Prizmo*, first take a picture of a document — such as a letter, syllabus, or lecture outline. Make sure to adjust the on-screen settings to heighten the picture's quality. Then, by using *Prizmo*'s built-in OCR, the image is rendered into text. *Prizmo*'s built-in text-to-speech then reads the document to you. Although designed for the iPhone, *Prizmo* can be used on an iPad. However, it is best to use an iDevice with at least a 5 megapixel camera.

Getting and Reading Audio Books

Many individuals with dyslexia prefer to read audiobooks. Audiobooks side step the difficulty of dealing with print. Also audiobooks generally are recorded by human narrators instead of using a robotic text-to-speech voice. Unfortunately, most academic books are not available as audiobooks, except those from Learning Ally.

Amazon's Audible

Audible is synonymous with audiobooks. They have over 100,000 audiobooks directly from publishers. Professional narrators, who provide one of the highest quality reading experiences around, read each audiobook. The audiobook selection varies from popular literary works — e.g. Alexander Dumas' *Three Musketeers* — to academic works — e.g. Edward Said's *Orientalism* — to lecture series — e.g. Great Courses and foreign language series. These audiobooks can be purchased individually online (Audible.com) or on a Kindle Fire. However, Audible also has a monthly subscription option: $14.95 for one book per month and $22.95 for two books per month. Purchased content can be accessed on the web, a Kindle Fire, or an Android/Apple mobile device. With Kindle or a mobile device you can change the listening speed rate of the audiobook between .7x and 3x. One advantage of an Audible account is that all your books are kept in a cloud library for you and hence can be re-downloaded on various devices at any time.

LibriVox Audiobooks

LibriVox (based on the Latin "vox libri" meaning "voice books") is an internet service where volunteers have made audio recordings of public-domain books. Public-domain books are those written before 1923. These include titles such as Mark Twain's The Adventures of *Huckleberry Finn* and J.M. Barrie's *Peter Pan.* Best of all, these audiobooks are free. A basic Audio books app on a Kindle Fire or Android/Apple mobile device easily accesses them. The *Audiobooks* app (part of Audiobooks.com) has searched the LibriVox collection to find the best recording to present to readers.

Learning Ally

Learning Ally is an organization that supplies audiobooks to print-impaired readers. You must provide documentation of your diagnosis of a print disability, like dyslexia, to use Learning Ally. Membership is $119 per year. Learning Ally primarily supplies textbooks and school-related books; they are a major source for audio textbooks. Their library contains over 75,000 titles. Mostly, volunteers read the books; thus, one audiobook may have more than one reader. Some books, though, are generated using text-to-speech voices. Moreover, some other books may also show the text while a narrator reads it. Learning Ally allows you to download these audiobooks onto an Android/Apple mobile device or a PC/Mac computer. The ability to carry around an entire set of textbooks in your pocket on a mobile device serves as a major advantage to the *Learning Ally mobile* app. Both Jim and Maria have used Learning Ally with great success. If you do not find a required book on Learning Ally, you can make a request that they record that book. Keep in mind that the decision whether they record it or not is ultimately up to them. Quick tip: I, Jim, found that if a textbook available in Learning Ally is only one revision behind the most current textbook that I physically have, listening to the older version while looking at the new version usually still works out. For example, if your class is using the 6th edition of United States History but you can only get audio access to the 5th edition, you will still be able to complete your readings without too much confusion or difference from the rest of the class. Also you can search the Learning Ally library to locate additional sources for your research. I, Jim, found a dozen books to read about dyslexia.

Audio-file Based on Text-to-speech

If you like the sound and consistent pace of a synthetic voice, then you may appreciate having an audiobook where it is the narrator. With your computer, an app, or a Kindle you can have the synthetic voice read what is written. However, certain software allows you to export a MP3 file where a synthetic voice reads the entire book. This is just like a normal audiobook only the narrator is the synthetic voice and not a human. *K3000* and *Premier Literacy* have this feature included within their suites. Bookshare also lets you download certain books as a MP3. This may be a nice option for you if you want a labor-free text-to-speech experience when you read.

Victor Reader Stream

Victor Reader Stream ($369) is a hand held reading device originally designed for blind or vision-impaired individuals. However, I, Jim, have found it very handy as a dyslexic reader. The Victor Reader does not have a screen. It closely mimics a high-quality mp3 player. However, Victor Reader can read text files like Word documents or Bookshare books using high quality built-in voices. Victor Reader can also play audio files from Learning Ally or *Audible*. The advantage of the Victor Reader is that it provides an audio experience while using a regular textbooks and books. In order to download content onto the device, a connection can be made wirelessly with Bookshare or Learning Ally and wired to a computer for other document files. You can easily place many text or audio files on this 4 oz. player for ease of access. Additionally, you can readily bookmark important passages for rereading. I used one of these for years. Although one could argue that many of the functions of a Victor Reader can be done on a smart phone, Victor Reader offers efficient file management and large storage for a multitude of audiobook and text files. It is great to carry all of your books on a device that fits into the palm of your hand.

Other Text-to-speech Readers

Claro Software

Claro offers a few different software options to aid individuals in reading and writing. Here follows a breakdown of the current software available from Claro:

ClaroRead [Mac and PC]

ClaroRead is an extremely useful tool for reading and writing. The software works as a floating toolbar. If you like, you can minimize the toolbar while continuing to read or dock the toolbar to the top of your computer screen. You can read text in almost any document format. ClaroRead has several highlighting options. When reading within the app, you can choose the familiar sentence and word highlighting option, or there is also the "trail highlighting" option. With trail highlighting, the current word being read is highlighted while trailing words remain highlighted. I, Jim, particularly like this method. Also, within documents the font color of the sentence being read can be changed. When reading outside the application — such as with *Firefox* — select a portion of text and that will initiate the reading. While in a *Microsoft Word* document, you can read using the focus sentence feature. Only the sentence being read is highly visible because the other sentences are dimmed. You can also easily change character and line spacing within a Word document from the *ClaroRead* toolbar for easier reading.

ClaroRead also comes with great writing features like a homophone detector, word prediction, and spell check. There is a set of excellent videos about *ClaroRead* on *YouTube* for you to get more information. *ClaroRead* comes in two incarnations: a basic version and a pro version. With the basic version ($99) you only can read text from outside applications. The pro version ($295) offers all the features listed above. *ClaroRead* is an exceptional program.

ClaroPDF [iOS]

ClaroPDF ($2.99) reads PDFs aloud on the iPad and functions very similarly to *ClaroRead*. *ClaroPDF* highlights both the sentence and word as it reads aloud. You can also change the font color of the text being read. Additionally, trail highlighting is available. *ClaroPDF* allows you to annotate your PDF. You can underline or highlight important parts of the text with different colored virtual markers. Moreover, you can add notes or draw shapes around text or graphic elements. *ClaroPDF* enables you to read and study PDFs handily on your iPad.

ReadIris [iOS]

ReadIris ($10.99) is a highly accurate OCR app for the iPad. If you receive a PDF that has inaccessible text, import the PDF into *ReadIris* and perform OCR to create a digitally readable text version of the original PDF on your iPad. Alternatively, just upload photos from your camera roll and *ReadIris* will process them. *ReadIris* can easily identify the difference between text and graphic elements of a document. Additionally, *ReadIris* will keep the integrity and format of the original document in your new digital text version.

GhostReader [Mac]

GhostReader imports Text, Word, HTML, PDF and RTF documents to be read. The interface is very customizable. You can change the text's color and font style; moreover, the text window can have different colored backgrounds and the highlight on text being read can be any color. Text imported into *GhostReader* can be converted into an audio file for iTunes. Also, you can change the speed right within the app; the adjustment is incremented in words per minute (WPM). More than just a document reader, *GhostReader* brilliantly reads text from almost any outside application. So when reading an article on *Safari* or a document on *Pages*, simply highlight a certain portion of the text and go to the "Service" settings (a sub-setting under the App's pulldown menu at the very top) and chose "Read Aloud with GhostReader" and that particular text will instantly pop-up within the *GhostReader* app screen.

Reading with *GhostReader* is a unique experience. You are able to edit the pronunciation of certain words in the settings, but, through the use of "tags," you are also able to do a host of other manipulations to the synthetic voice to make your reading experience ideal. Tags operate by literally tagging parts of your text with a specific command, i.e. "Read this sentence at 180 wpm not 300 wpm." Of course, the commands are not given verbally but programmed into the the tag's specific feature. There are many tag options including: changing the speed rate, synthetic voice, language spoken, and volume; adding a moment of silence; and making the synthetic voice spell out the word.

I, Maria, find this tagging feature revolutionizes my reading of journal articles or heavy scholarly material. Often scholars, versed in many languages, directly quote foreign articles or include primary quotations in a modern or ancient foreign language. Employing a synthetic voice often ruins the experience of reading a multilingual article; the voice will just try to read the French, let's say, with English phonetics. With tagging, you can "tag" a quotation as French or German or what have you, and then *GhostReader* will change the synthetic voice to one for that language just for the length of that quotation and then immediately go back to reading in English. Additionally, you could also tag the sentence to be read more slowly, something I would do when using foreign language tags since I am not fluent enough in foreign languages to hear them as fast as English.

Explore these tagging features for yourself. It is priced at $40. I believe this is one of the best text reading softwares for Mac. My only complaint is that it lacks a

Daisy book reader to enable you to import Bookshare books.

Kurzweil 3000 Professional [Mac and PC]

Kurzweil 3000 (*K3000*) can import many document file types, including documents created using their scan features (discussed further in the scanning books section). As you read your document, *K3000* highlights the sentence or words being read. You may change your document — such as a book chapter — into audio MP3 files, if you desire. The "study skills" toolbar enables you to add annotations; these include highlighting or typing a note onto text itself. Wonderfully, *K3000* can read back to you the highlights you made previously. Additionally, your highlights and notes can be extracted and changed into a MP3 file. All of these features are a part of the larger *K3000* software package selling for over one thousand dollars.

NaturalReader [Mac and PC]

NaturalReader reads document files or selected text from outside applications aloud within their text reader app. It is available for free and offers several different features, making it a great program. With the free version, you can import TXT or RTF files to be read. Additionally, NaturalReader also has a handy floating toolbar, which you can use to read text taken from almost any outside app stored on your clipboard. Just select some text from a document or webpage and click on the play/read button to start the reading. Once the text is imported, while the programs reads that text both the sentence and the individual word are highlighted, a very smart and helpful way to keep your place. Mind you, all of this is for free!

NaturalReader also comes in paid versions for $69, $129, and $199 with both the free features and additional ones. The paid version will import Word, HTML, RTF, TEXT, and PDF documents. The documents open in the NaturalReader window. However, for Word documents, you can use the Word plug-in to read within Word itself. Once the document file is inside the *NaturalReader* app, though, you can then export the reading as an audio file. Further, some additional high quality voices and a hot key to start the reading are available. Thus, the paid version is comparable to *Premier Literacy's Universal Reader Plus* and *GhostReader*. The most expensive version includes an OCR scanner.

Premier Literacy

When purchasing software from Premier Assistive, you can buy each piece of software individually or as part of a bundle. The bundled software is called the Literacy Productivity Pack. You may feel put off by the use of "literacy" in the title, but Premier Assistive sells a lot of software to K-12 education, so the Pack's name reflects that market. Despite this, the software bundle is very useful for college students. The *Literacy Productivity*

Pack includes 10 separate pieces of software: *Worksheet Wizard, Write Now, Scan and Read Pro, Talking Word Processor, PDF Equalizer, Text-to-do Audio, e-Text Reader, Universal Reader Plus, English Talking Dictionary,* and *Talking Calculator. The PDF Equalizer, Talking Word Processor,* and *Universal Reader Plus* remain the three most useful programs. The overall user interface for each piece of software has a similar look and feel across applications and OS interfaces. The Pack is available for PC and Mac, though at this time it performs significantly better on PC. Of course, by buying these pieces of software together in the bundle you save money; the Literacy Productive Pack sells for $249.95.

PDF Equalizer

PDF Equalizer is a great program for reading and studying PDF documents. We rated this program 5 stars below mostly due to its good note-taking features integrated well with the text reader itself. *PDF Equalizer* can read the whole PDF continuously or a section at a time. The continuous mode does not highlight words or sentences as it reads. If you select a portion, then a smaller second window will open and in that screen words are highlighted as text is read aloud. Further, font size and color, as well as background color, can be changed in this second reading window. The program can also extract the PDF text and then create a MP3 file, which you can carry to many different devices.

The notes and the highlight marker features provide the biggest benefit to using PDF Equalizer. Within the app each page of the PDF has an associated "notes" page. You can make notes and excerpt text — this is handy for later studying. You can also highlight the text on the screen with one of four different color highlight options. You can restrict the reading to only these highlighted passages. So, when reviewing the PDF, you can just read your highlights.

A very unique feature of this software is the "summarization" tool: Language Model Information Summarization. This tool searches your PDF for the important points and excerpts them onto a different page. You can set how much summarization you want to do, say 25% or 30%. For more information, seek out the video series on YouTube expanding on *PDF Equalizer*. *PDF Equalizer* by itself costs $99.95; alternatively, you can receive the software through purchasing the Pack.

Universal Reader Plus

Universal Reader Plus can read aloud selected text from almost any document. It is an extremely helpful and easy-to-use tool. After you select text, click the red button on the floating tool bar to start the reading. Text is displayed in a window attached to the toolbar. This is true both for PC and Mac. You may wonder why a Mac user would use this program since it is similar to built-in "select and speak" on the Mac. The text opening in a separate customizable window shows the utility of this app. The text in the window can be specialized to your needs — you can adjust the font size and color of the text and background color of the window. Like most good text readers, the words are highlighted as they are read. This software also contains Premier Assistive's summarization tool.

A very good feature of the PC version of this software is the "Talking Pointer." You can read almost any text just by hovering your cursor over it. This is especially handy for reading webpages. The *Universal Reader Plus* costs $79.95 or can be purchased as part of the Literacy Productive Pack. This software has similar features to that of *ClaroRead, NaturalReader,* and *GhostReader*, but with the purchase of the Pack you automatically have *Universal Reader Plus*.

Speak Selection [Apple iOS and OSX]

Speak Selection reads only specifically highlighted groups of words. It is very handy. Instead of toggling VoiceOver on and off, you can select a sentence or paragraph and have the iDevice or Mac computer read aloud to you only that passage. On iOS devices, you select and highlight a word by simply double tapping on it; then touch one of the anchor points and drag to select all the text you wish to read. You can also triple tap on a word to select the paragraph. After you make the selection, a menu will pop up with "Speak" as an option.

For computer, right click the highlighted sentence and choose the "speak" option. When you initiate Speak on either device, that selected text is read aloud.

Subtext [iOS]

The *Subtext* app enables you to access Google's 4 million ebooks (2 million of which are in the public domain). Best of all, the app has a very pleasant voice to read the books aloud. The speed of the voice can be adjusted in the *Subtext* settings after you open a book. Unfortunately, *Subtext* requires a yearly $30 subscription fee to access the read-aloud function; up to 10 individuals can share this subscription.

TextAloud [PC]

TextAloud for the PC is an inexpensive ($29.95) and handy reading tool. For years, I, Jim, used this as my primary way to read on the PC. *TextAloud* reads any text copied to the clipboard. In fact, you can set the preferences to read any copied text automatically. This versatility is very helpful when proofreading your writing. When reading in this manner you have the option of having the selected text read in the *TextAloud* window or not. I find reading in the window helpful, since the font color and background color can be changed to suit my preferences. Word, RTF and PDF files can be imported into *TextAloud*.

There are also plug-ins for *Word, Internet Explorer,* and *Firefox*, which add a reading button to these programs for easy reading aloud. Reading, of course, is done with high quality text-to-speech voices. *TextAloud* especially shines in producing audio files of text within their app window. I often create an audiobook of my Bookshare books. I create a MP3 file with *TextAloud* for each chapter in the book to be read using my iPhone or iPod Touch. This app offers ease and utility, making it a great choice as a reader aid on a PC.

@Voice Aloud Reader [Android and Kindle Fire]

@Voice Aloud Reader reads imported articles from webpages or directly from *Pocket* and *Instapaper*. Once you bring up a web article, select the share icon to send it to *@Voice Aloud Reader*. *@Voice Aloud Reader* will then extract the main article and display the text within their app. You can customize the font size, select day or night reading mode, and change the rate of reading speed (the voice is taken from the device OS). The convenience and ease of use of this app make it a great choice for reading articles on mobile devices.

VoiceOver [iOS and OSX]

VoiceOver is the built-in screen reader in iOS and Mac computers. Voiceover reads on-screen options and text to you; it can be turned on and off in Settings or

System Preferences. When VoiceOver is operating on an iDevice, you control it by special gestures: two finger swipe down for continuous reading of an article or book, three finger swipe right or left to turn pages, and double tap to select items. Using the Accessibility Shortcuts provides a simpler way to control whether VoiceOver is in operation. When you set up Accessibility Shortcut in iOS Settings, a triple click of the home button will ask you if you want to turn VoiceOver on or off. The accessibility feature "Rotor" gesture supplies additional VoiceOver options with a simple hand flick. The Rotor gesture is akin to turning a knob: you put two fingers on the screen and then turn them as if you were turning a knob. The gesture provokes a small circular-shape options window to appear, which you can then rotate through the rotor options. Helpful rotor options include speech rate, volume, and zoom. Reading speed and rotor options for VoiceOver can be managed in the Settings. Youtube offers demonstrative videos of VoiceOver, Rotor gestures, and Accessibility Shortcut.

Using a Kindle Fire

Amazon's Kindle Fire tablet has become one of our favorite ways to read. The Kindle Fire HD 6 is just $99 and the HD 7 is available for $139. These prices are unbeatable! The Amazon Kindle bookstore has over 2 million ebooks. Almost all of these books can be read using the high-quality text-to-speech voice built into the

Kindle Fire (note: neither Kindle Paperwhite nor Voyager come with this feature). The process to access this text-to-speech is superior to that of iDevices, which force you to use VoiceOver. VoiceOver on iDevices and TalkBack on Android devices were designed for blind individuals to navigate and to read on mobile devices. When you want to read aloud on iDevices or Android devices you must turn on the screen reader for the device. Once turned on, the screen reader reads everything on screen. Operating the reading is more difficult with screen readers turned on. With the Kindle Fire, though, one does not have to mimic blind users in order to read books aloud; this is a big advantage. When you read a book you turn on the text-to-speech within the book. A simple tap on a play/ stop button starts or stops reading.

Kindle eBooks

Kindle Fire reads any AZW3 (Kindle book) file. Amazon Kindle bookstore remains the best place to find Kindle ebooks. This is due to their large selection, including ample free titles, and professionally-made books with active tables of contents and footnotes. Certainly, all books bought on Amazon are stored on the cloud and can be re-downloaded onto the Kindle Fire at any time. However, Kindle books may also be found on a host of different websites. For example, Gutenberg and Archive.org are ideal places to find good-quality free older Kindle ebooks. Moreover, you may upload home-made Kindle books — using *Scrivener* or a book file converter — to your Kindle Fire. I, Maria, quite frequently transform my scanned books or articles into Kindle books. Quick tip: I use the app *Calibre* to convert EPUB files (another ebook file extension) into AZW3 files. This is a free computer application that allows you to convert several formats and to edit the "metadata," which enables you to add a book cover or indicate the author. Needless to say, Kindle Fire offers ample flexibility in choosing your book library.

Organization

After you have a good collection of ebooks, you may want to organize them. In your virtual bookshelf you are able to sort your books by: recent, title, and author. However, I am especially fond of Kindle's "Collections" feature to organize my books. Simply put, this feature serves as a book folder system. Your Collections can be accessed in your bookshelf window through the extra-features pop-out on the far-left side. When I open my collections I see a series of boxes, with small thumbnail previews of books inside and titles above each box. I can label the boxes however I wish. I tap the box to open it and then larger thumbnail previews of books show up and I just tap any book to open it. The ability to see the book-sleeve within the box/folder helps me to find the book I want more easily. Naming the boxes whatever I want also aids my categorization of what I own. Past these options, I am able to store books in more than one box. Lewis Carroll's *Alice in Wonderland* is both a "classic" and a "juvenile" book; with Collections, I can label it as both. Lastly, I can showcase any of my collections on the home-screen for quick access. I like to have my "currently reading" and "Latin" folder on my home-screen. You can make your Collections as extensive or narrow as you desire and just make them help you get to your books faster.

Reading

After you download an ebook onto your Kindle Fire, open the book. A one-finger tap in the middle of the book page will bring up the book option menu. Tap on the "Aa" to bring up the view adjustments options. On this pop-up window you will see "more settings" at the bottom. Tap on "more settings" to bring up a menu where you can turn text-to-speech on. Now when you return to your book, tap in the middle of the screen and see that a play/pause button is visible in the lower left corner of your book. Tap on this play button to begin text-to-speech reading. While the voice reads aloud, pages will automatically be turned when the voice comes to the end of a page. You can pause the reading at any time by manually flipping the page or tapping the pause button on the book menu screen. Reading speed can be adjusted within the book menu screen with a tap of the speedometer symbol in the lower right hand corner. Reading speeds range from .7x to 4x;

the 1x reading speed indicates the reading pace at which most people read aloud.

"Immersion reading" stands out as one of the great advantages of the Kindle Fire. With the purchase of certain ebooks, Amazon offers you the privilege of purchasing the accompanying audiobook at a reduced price. For example, with the purchase of the ebook Mark Twain's *Adventures of Tom Sawyer* for 99¢, you can purchase the audiobook at the reduced rate of 99¢. When the ebook and audiobook are paired (note: make sure you buy the audiobook on the ebook purchase page to ensure this pairing), the narration comes from the audiobook instead of from the text-to-speech voice. Additionally, the text is highlighted during the narration (that is not the case for text-to-speech reading).

Side Load Apps

Many Android apps are not in the Amazon App Store. Several of these apps can be purchased and "side loaded" onto the Kindle Fire. This is my, Jim's, method for loading these apps onto my Kindle Fire: First, go to "Settings" and scroll down to "Applications." After opening Applications, turn on "Apps from Unknown Sources." Next, install the app APK Extractor onto your Android. With this app you will be able to transfer an app's APK installation files to your Kindle Fire. To do this, open APK Extractor on your Android. You will be presented a list of your apps. You can find the GoRead app, previously downloaded by you, on the list. Press and hold the GoRead app name. Emailing the APK file will be one of the options that pops up. Choose this option and email the APK to your Kindle. Open the email on your Kindle, tap the attached APK file. Kindle will then take you to an install window. Go through the necessary options on this pop-up screen to install the app on your Kindle. After installation, you can find your app in the apps section of your Kindle (note: You need to look under apps "on device" to locate the app).

You can also install free android apps by going to the: 1Mobil.com website. This site allows you to download their app on your Kindle, which enables you to access many free Android apps like *YouTube* and the *Chrome* browser. A very good video on this process is found at the www.kindleforkids.com website.

Some individuals "root" their Kindle Fire in order to get the Google Play Store on their Kindle. I strongly advise against this. By rooting your Kindle Fire, you void your warranty. I have found that almost all apps I need are in the Amazon App Store. Two exceptions include the *GoRead* app and the *Learning Ally* app to support reading. However, I successfully transferred both of these apps to my Kindle Fire from my Android smartphone with the process described above.

Bringing Bookshare eBooks to Kindle

We have talked a lot about the advantages of Bookshare ebooks and using the Kindle to read ebooks. Why not then put Bookshare ebooks on the Kindle! There is a process involved to actually move these ebooks to a Kindle. I, Maria, will describe it here based on doing it successfully with my Mac, several times.

1. Download the *Daisy* file (a zip folder) of your chosen book from bookshare.org. You can do so by clicking "download," which is one of the options when you view a book. The Daisy file is the only one which will download to your computer when you do this. It downloads as a zip file which automatically expands to a folder with the Daisy files.

2. Within your finder there will be a folder (pre-named the title of your chosen book) with several files within it, each with uncommon extensions. Highlight the file with the extension ".xml."

3. Open this file with *TextEdit* (*NotePad* on PC). The content will be in HTML.

4. With the *TextEdit* file still open on your computer, open the same .xml file again with *Safari* (*Internet Explorer* or *Firefox*). You do not need internet for this to open. This should look like a normal Bookshare ebook page: the title and copyright information.

5. Select all the text within the webpage. Please use the shortcut command (Mac: command + A; PC: ctrl + A)

to do this because it will be too difficult manually. Now copy this text.

6. Open *Word* and paste the text within the text file. This will take some time as the file will be numerous pages.

7. Save the text file as ".txt" (if you are using *Pages*, save it as ".epub").

8. You will now need to convert that file to ".AZW3" (or ".mobi"). You can find the converter of your choice online. I have found *Calibre* to be very good. This app is free and allows you to add a book cover and metadata. After you make the conversion, have the Kindle file at the ready on your desktop.

9. With a purchase of a Kindle, a cord comes that enables you to connect the device to any computer. Make this connection. (Note: Mac users will need to download the free *Android File Transfer* app first.) A window will pop up which includes all the files on the Kindle. Now, simply carry-transfer your new book into the "Books" folder of your Kindle. Within minutes it will appear on your inner-device carousel.

CHAPTER 7 - Tackling the Writing Challenge

Writing and College

Expressing oneself in clear coherent writing is essential to college success. Writing draws on a number of skills. One must be able to investigate a subject area and organize one's thoughts about the subject. After organizing thoughts and conclusions, one must then express them in coherent sentences. This assumes appropriate spelling and grammar and valid sentence structure. Often, however, students with dyslexia have difficulty doing this. Many dyslexic students have what is called "written expression learning disorder" or dysgraphia.

Very often difficulties with written expression are more pronounced than difficulties with reading. Both authors of this book have difficulties with written expression. I, Jim, have learned to compensate for both reading and writing difficulties; however, writing remains the most difficult area for me to succeed at. I, Maria, have to revise my papers many, many times to fix mistakes. I even have to have others look at my writing to make sure that I have not missed finding mistakes.

Here are indications that a college student like yourself may have difficulties with written expression:

• You dislike writing and writing assignments.

- You have difficulty organizing your thoughts into a structured outline.
- You struggle to translate your thoughts onto paper.
- You often write incomplete or run-on sentences.
- You get confused about what verb tense to use.
- You are not sure how to spell a word you want to use in your writing.
- You tend to use the same adjective or noun repeatedly.
- You use the verb "to be" more often than an action verb.
- You cannot properly proofread your work because you cannot see your mistakes.
- Your writing seems disconnected and does not flow easily from one idea to another.

Jim's Three Tricks to Improve Your Writing

When I, Jim, was in graduate school I had trouble getting my Master's thesis proposal accepted. My writing was not up to thesis writing standards. I approached one of my professors who helped undergraduate psychology majors with writing and asked him for assistance. He met with me twice a week for a semester going over my proposal. He stressed removing jargon and textbook-style language from my writing. He had three principles that he stressed to improve my writing: simple sentences, simple language, and simple logic. Simple sentences are best. People with dyslexia (or dysgraphia) often have difficulty writing a good sentence. Dyslexics can think about ideas but have difficulty getting the ideas written down. Frequently, thoughts are not written down as complete sentences. Alternatively, one very long run-on sentence may end up being an entire paragraph. Writing can be improved by understanding sentences. Sentences are made up of a subject and a predicate. Here are two sentences.

1. John spoke lovingly to his mother.

The subject is "John." The predicate is "spoke lovingly to his mother."

2. Abraham Lincoln was president during the American Civil War.

The subject is "Abraham Lincoln." The predicate is "was president during the American Civil War."

Simple sentences are clear. Simple sentences get ideas across. Sentences with combined ideas can be confusing. So, simple is best, especially when one is improving one's writing.

Simple language is best. People generally learn to write in school. In forming a written work you often imitate existing written works that you have already read. However, dyslexics often do not read a lot. Dyslexics most often read textbooks. Surprisingly, textbooks are often not good examples of writing. Textbooks are often ponderous to read. They are dry due to their overuse of specialized language — jargon — and lack of vivid descriptions. Good writing reads like a conversation.

Good writing, when spoken aloud, sounds like someone talking to someone else.

Simple logic is best. A discourse is commendable when ideas flow from one idea to the next. Writing works the same way. To make your writing flow logically, follow this method. You start by writing a list of your ideas. Each idea is expressed by just one word or maybe three words. You then rearrange your word list so ideas flow from one to another. Put your ideas on note cards to make the rearranging easier and more tactile for you. Writing usually has a beginning, a middle, and an end section, so you should arrange your list into a beginning, a middle, and an end. At first, writing has gaps in the logical steps. As you look over your list, add additional logical steps. By the end you should be able to answer how your points connect with each other. You then can arrange your ideas into similar groups to make paragraphs. Lastly, you write a simple sentence for each of your ideas. Before you know it, you have written your paper.

What's improved my, Jim's, writing?

Three things made me a better writer. First, I got help from excellent writers in tutoring me about my own writing. Secondly, I participated in some extensive writing projects like my master's thesis and my doctoral dissertation. Third, I read about a subject area to get the background that I needed to spur my writing. For a number of years I have had an interest in the subjects of reading and writing. You can say that I wanted to know more about that area I found so difficult and others found much easier.

I have read a number of books on the history and theory of reading. I have long been fascinated with the history of books and print, so I've read a great deal about Gutenberg and the printing press. More recently I have done a good deal of reading on the subject of writing. One of my favorite authors in this area is Mary Leonhardt and her book *99 Ways to Get Kids to Love Writing*. She was an English teacher for many years. Her number one principle for getting kids to love writing is to get them reading. She says over and over again that the best way to improve someone's writing is to get them reading.

I suppose all of the reading that I have done has helped me become a better writer. But I must admit that the world of words is still somewhat of a mystery to me. Good writers will often say that they enjoy the style of someone's writing or they like the words that people choose. I don't have such epiphanies when I read someone's writing. As I read, I am simply glad to get the knowledge that someone has written down for me to understand. So I do recommend that people read and hopefully this will help them write. At least this is what the experts say. But my first recommendation is, if you want to improve your writing, find someone who can help you with your writing.

There is a basic principle that if you want to get better at something you have to practice it. For me, doing a master's thesis and the doctoral dissertation were my practice in writing. When I did each of these projects, I had to write and rewrite and rewrite what I had written. Also each of these projects lasted for many semesters, not just one project for a class. The greatest value of doing my projects was to understand the importance of rewriting. The other major thing I learned was to spot when I needed to expand on my subject in order to communicate well to my reader. I also learned how to make transitions from one paragraph to another or from one subject thought to another subject thought. All of this took a great deal of time and effort, and amounted to a great deal of practice.

Lastly, what helps me with my writing is to read about a subject area before I start writing. There are some people who seem to be able to pull the words out of nowhere and just put them down on the paper. I am not one of these individuals. When I had to write for my freshman composition class, I would sometimes spend 20 hours a week on forming a paragraph to turn in. I remember walking into a classmate's dorm room one half hour before he had to turn in his essay, and he simply sat down and whipped it out, no revisions or anything, and he got straight A's. I still struggle with my writing today. I find if I have writer's block I usually have to go read about a subject area first in order to tank up on information to be able to get past the block. So these are my three approaches to writing: first get some help, practice what you want to achieve, and tank up on information.

Maria's Writing Method

Writing is not very natural for me. I enjoy sharing information through writing. I even — dare I say it — like to write papers and assignments! However, I get quite nervous when I write and I often write very clumsily. Writing can be compared to walking. Some write with the effortlessness of walking across a room or even walking a few miles. Some, though, have to think and try so hard when they write that it feels like walking with weights or having to think before every step. This second feeling is what I experience when I write. You can see now my internal conflict between wanting to express myself through writing but finding it difficult to do so. I have found ways to write and write well despite my difficulties, and I want to share them here.

First, I am what one might consider an overly-organized person. I need everything to fit in the right place and to have everything neatly organized to function well. I carry this fastidiousness over to my writing. I will not write word one until I have an outline in extreme detail ready.

There are different kinds of outlines. Mind-mapping enables you to put thoughts, lists, and even pictures into bubbles and make connections between them with arrows. This is highly effective in the beginning stages to show larger connections between ideas and to brainstorm different perspectives on an issue. A structured formal outline with bullet points and indentions is most beneficial for the final organization of ideas. This structured outline is my "go-to" when preparing for a paper.

In my outline I include short sentences or even just keywords that take the place of what will be full sentences and paragraphs in my paper. Below those I store evidence and detailed information. I like to color-code my outlines both to help me navigate them and also to help see how my paper is taking shape. I put all primary quotations or paraphrases in one color and all secondary information in another. I leave my original interpretations and thoughts in black. I strive for an abundance of black because I want my voice to be heard in the paper.

Outlines vary in length and detail. I tend toward the enthusiastic side, so mine are quite long. For example, I was in a class once where the teacher asked for an outline right before the first draft was due. The end paper was supposed to be about seven pages (mine ended up being fourteen pages). Most students brought in a two page barebones outline. I brought in a ten page very detailed outline. Not everyone has to put in as much detail as I do, but I find it is very helpful when I start writing. Everything I want to say and include is right there, already written out and organized. All I need to do is add the sentences and paragraphs to fill out the outline information. This pre-planning also helps me to focus on my sentences when I write. I do not have to over-tax myself with organizing information and writing; I can just focus on writing!

Second, I find it helpful to increase the sophistication of my writing as I rewrite. Starting to write is by far one of the hardest steps when forming a paper. Hesitation and nervousness well up inside me and no energy is left for the actual writing. I feel this way often. I say to myself that I cannot write as well as others or I am going to get frustrated. I figured out that I was trying to write perfectly the first time. Previously, I was writing in ink and nothing could be changed or erased. This does not have to be true! Now, I write on a computer so I can change anything I want. I often leave myself days to finish an assignment, so I can wait until tomorrow to reread and rewrite. This realization made way for a better writing process. Armed with my outline, I sit down at my desk (or comfortable chair) and tell myself that I will write anything I can based on the outline for as long as I can. This is an adaptation of something called "free writing." Words keep appearing on the screen as I press myself to type until I just cannot anymore. By the time I have finished, I have made a good start at writing my paper. I then go back and rewrite sentences to make them sound better. I can go back again to edit the grammar. The pressures of perfection are off and in their place is a method to layer on sophistication.

Lastly, I have just alluded to this; I do multiple drafts. I know that I cannot write perfectly the first time. I start an assignment at least a week to three days before it is due. Once I have a full draft I go back to read and revise up to three more times. I have my dad look at the first draft and he shows me my grammar mistakes. One time as I re-read it, my goal may be to shorten the sentences and take out passive constructions. Another time may be to look at my scholarly content and see if all the facts are right and if I paraphrased secondary authors correctly. Since writing and editing are not natural for me, I stagger my duties as much as I can so that I am left with small, easy-to-accomplish tasks. After completing my outline, free-writing, and multiple drafts, I know what I am submitting is the best I can do!

Word Processing and Media Processing

Today most people use a computer to store documents and a keyboard to physically write the document. However, some college students may not be fully informed what a "word processor" is, nor have been taught keyboarding skills in a classroom. So let us explain about "word processing." Word processing is writing on a computer. The most often used word processors are Microsoft *Word, Word Perfect,* Apple *Pages,* or Google *Docs.*

Writing with a word processor is different than writing on paper or with a typewriter. Since the document is digital, everything you type is not permanent — the whole document is pliable. You can delete words or sentences. One of the major editing practices when writing is to move sentences or words from one place to another. This practice is called copy and paste or cut and paste. Word processing programs also offer the ability to format the style of the text in special ways. Text size or color can be changed. When emphasis is needed, text can be made bold, italicized, or underlined. Although originally document formatting was restricted to what could be produced on tangible paper, today you can format documents in countless ways and still print them with advances in printer technology. However, there is a new trend toward not printing documents at all but keeping them in a digital format. When no physical paper is involved, you can create versatile documents with clickable web links, photographs, video clips, graphs, and even music.

Editing

After you finish writing a work the logical next step is to edit the writing. Dyslexia can greatly hinder your ability to edit. I, Maria, know when I read my work myself it is just as laborious as reading *Jane Austin*, so it goes slowly and inaccurately. I read what I want to see and not what is really there more often than not. Since I also have dysgraphia, I find that I get confused about the grammar structure and how I organized my ideas in the sentence. How do I edit what I write then? I do several things and look at the text from several different perspectives to try to find as many mistakes as I can. Here are some that many dyslexics have employed.

First, read what you write using the synthetic voice. This tool is more fully explained above as it is also helpful for sentence elaboration. Just as if your parents or your teacher read it, this enables you to hear what you truly wrote, instead of what you thought you wrote. Done at a slow pace, this method will certainly illuminate mistakes in any written work.

Second, take it one sentence at a time. Isolate a sentence in your paragraph and just think about its makeup without trying to overburden your mind with a whole paragraph of sentences. All your attention and focus on just one sentence will allow you to see the structure of the sentence more easily and, by extension, any mistakes therein.

Third, make a style sheet to direct and inform your editing process. I, Maria, took this idea from the example of some of my professors and have edited it slightly to present here. This style sheet has two sections: Macro-Aspects and Micro-Aspects.

The Macro-Aspects deal with features that make up the paper as a whole. Here is a list:
- Professor's rubric
- Formatting considerations (often the professor will specify how many words he wants or if you can use section headers and so on)
- Font, font size, page margin, block quote indention specifications, etc.
- A list of difficult names and words you will use in your paper repeatedly (e.g. Mediterranean or Sigmund Freud)

The Micro-Aspects are especially useful when editing the body of the paper. These considerations will aid you to look for something specific, rather than just what looks or sounds wrong. Here are just some examples:
- Indirect Statements (adding the "that")
- Repetitive adjectives/adverbs
- Changing "it is" or "this is" to active verbs and specific subjects
- Correct use of commas
- Number and tense agreement

Lastly, use tools and resources to help highlight key parts of your text. Some of the most beneficial editing tools are found right within the word processor itself. Almost every word processor, including Microsoft *Word* and Apple *Pages*, have a Grammar and Spell Checker.

Use them to detect misspelled words and potential grammar mistakes. However, be extremely cautious when you are given suggestions about grammar and even spelling mistakes. You may be right. These tools help highlight potential errors but make sure you make the final decision whether it was a mistake or not. A great example is foreign words. Your dictionary will be set to English, but a French or Latin word may find its way into your document. The spell checker will say the word is misspelled but, in reality, it may just be a correctly spelled foreign word. Despite these rare situations, grammar and spell checker are very useful tools in the beginning stages of the editing process.

A program to highlight parts of speech, or syntactical elements, in your writing will do wonders for your editing. For example, if someone highlighted all the adjectives in your written work then you could see easily if you used the same one over and over. *iA Writer Pro* (iOS and OS X) can highlight the parts of speech: nouns, verbs, adjectives, adverbs, etc. This program retails around $20 but is very beneficial because of this tool. A free syntax highlighter is found on writersdiet.com. Called the "Writer's Diet Test" you put in a portion of your document and it will highlight the syntactical elements and even evaluate your writing based on them. If you use too many occurrences of "it is," it will tell you. The creator, Helen Sword, has helped academic writers with her books, including *Stylish Academic Writing*. So often trying to read your own writing becomes difficult because you cannot see the elements that make up a sentence, but these two programs can help with that greatly.

Scrivener's "split screen" and "snapshots" features can help you edit your paper. Split screen enables you to have two text windows open beside each other in one application. One screen can be your outline and the other your paper draft. By seeing both at the same time without hassle you are more free to concentrate on writing. This split screen can be useful in the editing process where you want to keep a close watch on your style chart. The snapshot feature helps you save earlier drafts or sections of drafts. Scrivener takes your current draft and turns it into a separate "snapshot." This snapshot can be saved. Your current editing document can be "rolled back" to your last snapshot at any time, which prevents concern of losing portions of text in the editing process. The ability to compare a snapshot with either your current editing document or another snapshot enables you to see the corrections you make.

Read & Write Gold has two beneficial editing features. The first feature highlights all the words in your paper that have an "evil twin" (K*urzweil 3000, Talking Word Processor, Write: OutLoud*). For example, it will highlight the word "effect" and on the side will list "affect" and a definition so you can choose the one best for your sentence. This will help you to be confident you chose the correct word, because spell check will not know what you meant to use, only that you spelled the word you wrote correctly or incorrectly. The second feature is a verb tense aid. You can put in any verb and it will give your a paradigm for that word so you can make sure the one you used is in the right tense. I would prefer that *Read & Write Gold* just highlight all the verbs, but this tool is still useful for tense accuracy.

I, Maria, want to give you a quick tip about using software for editing, like *Read & Write Gold* or *iA Writer Pro*. Instead of editing your work in the application window, do the final edits in your personal word processing program. The application window may strip your document of indentions and text formatting, so keep it just as a reference window. Make sure all edits happen on the final document instead of a copy you pasted into an application.

Getting Writing Help

You are not alone in writing assignments and papers. A lot of support is out there to help you succeed in your writing. This support comes in different forms. Physically, you can go to your college's Writing Center. Helpful students are there to assist you to see your own mistakes in grammar. I, Maria, was very lucky to have my dad's help at home. You may know an aspiring English teacher or someone in your own family willing to work with you on your writing. Also, you can try to submit an earlier draft of your work to the professor himself. If you are unsure about the accuracy of your facts or the clarity of your reasoning, this step may help "iron out" those issues before the professor has to attach a grade to your assignment. In addition to this in-person support there are many technological assistive softwares that can help you write and edit your work. What follows in the next section is the breakdown of those software options.

Conclusion

In college there will be a lot of writing, but you can do it! Learn what ways are best for you to write and feel comfortable doing so. Know you are not alone but have plenty of both in-person and technological help to aid your success. Understand that thoroughly editing your work yourself is possible, but you can always ask for help so you are comfortable with the result. Most importantly, get ready to experience that feeling of success and accomplishment when you finish your writing assignments with confidence!

CHAPTER 8 - Assistive Terminology with Word Processing

Word Prediction

There are a number of specialized word processors that help students with dyslexia write. These programs offer word prediction, word completion, and auditory feedback of words and sentences typed. Some programs that include this technology are K*urzweil 3000, Talking Word Processor, Write: OutLoud,* and *Read&Write Gold.* Word prediction supplies a list of words in a drop down window. Those words are the predicted words based on what you have typed. As you type the beginning of a word the prediction routine will guess nine or more possibilities of what is being typed. Usually the first two letters of a word will generate the correct word within the prediction window. Predictions are based on spelling and syntax and also how frequently a word is used. The major advantage of word prediction is to help you complete the spelling of words. For example, if you type "acess" The word prediction will provide the correct spelling "access." In fact, after you type just "ac", "access" will more than likely show up in the prediction list.

iOS 8 keyboards: QuickType keyboard in iOS 8 brings word prediction and next word prediction enhancements to Apple's standard keyboard. No matter which app you are using, the keyboard gives you word predictions. iOS 8 allows additional keyboard support beyond the Apple keyboard. This means keyboards that offer swype input with word completion are available system wide on your iDevice. Jim's favorite is Nuance's *Swype* keyboard. You run your finger across the letters of the keyboard in order to type. The keyboard is very good at interpreting swipes to words. Also it is great at correcting spelling.

Auditory Feedback

Auditory feedback is another benefit of these programs. You can have each sentence read back after you complete it. You can also highlight several sentences, paragraphs, or pages which are then read back to you. We both prefer to have paragraphs read back to us rather than one sentence at a time. Auditory feedback allows you to find problems within sentences, like wrong verb tenses, or to spot areas needing more elaboration. When you find yourself stuck on a paragraph, often reading it over several times will spark more creativity and a few more needed sentences.

Conquering Spelling

When I, Jim, went to my University, I was an extremely poor speller and writer. I had to learn how to improve my spelling, grammar, and written expression. With spell checker and speech recognition software, you might wonder, "why worry about spelling?" There is a good reason. When you improve your spelling, your writing will become easier and more fluid. If you are constantly asking yourself how to spell the next word, this slows down the creative process.

Often when trying to spell a word you say to yourself "If I can write it down then I can get it." This nice little trick is relying on your motor memory to help you spell. I, Jim, also remember my PIN numbers by motor memory.

As you frequently type words, the pattern of keystrokes becomes part of your motor memory and automatic. Hence, when you think of a word like "the," you do not think of the individual letters, but your fingers automatically generate the pattern for "the." You can combine this automaticity to help improve your spelling. As words you need help with pop-up in the prediction window, type out the entire word to cement it in your motor memory.

While taking a test you may or may not be able to use a computer. If you are not able to use a computer, you should see if you are able to use a dictionary to look up the spelling of words. A very good way to learn spelling is to look words up in a dictionary. At first this can be difficult. You might have to try three or four alternative spellings until you find the right one. But over time you will get better at guessing the spelling of a word. These guesses add up to learning the logic of spelling. Outside of a test, you may want to buy a dictionary app or ebook. Having a digital dictionary will help speed up your lookup time. You can quickly search for at least part of the word (the rest may come up in a suggestion) or tap to that letter in the alphabet rather than thumbing to find it. The less awkward it is for you to look up words, the more beneficial it will be for you.

Talking Your Way to Writing

Speech recognition or speech-to-text allows you to write by dictating your thoughts. Most current smartphones, tablets, and computers — such as PCs or Macs — have dictation built into them. Writing with pen and paper or keyboard is difficult; speaking often comes more naturally. Speech recognition sidesteps constantly thinking about how to spell words. Additionally, for dyslexics, speaking vocabulary is generally larger than spelling vocabulary. Thus, more words are available for writing.

At first, dictating is awkward. Writing is often more than simply talking to the computer. Writing frequently involves some extra composing of your thoughts in your mind before you speak. Practice leads to greater proficiency. I, Jim, rehearse a sentence that I am to write by saying it in my mind before I speak the sentence. Nuance's *Dragon NaturallySpeaking* for Windows or *Dragon Dictate* for Mac have many built-in commands. For example, punctuation for a sentence must be spoken, such as saying "comma," "period," or "question mark." Words in a sentence can be capitalized by saying "Cap" before the word. All these commands combined with writing can be a bit confusing. But after awhile, inserting the punctuation and other commands becomes almost automatic. By focusing on one sentence at a time, you can reduce some of the initial confusion. If a sentence contains several commands, I think through the commands several times before dictating. Dictation is a unique way of writing, but dictation and commands become much easier to do with practice. *Dragon NaturallySpeaking* and *Dragon Dictate* lets you control your computer by voice. For example, you can say "save document" to save your documents. There are literally hundreds of commands. It is difficult to learn so many commands, but you can start by learning the most frequent commands like "Save," "Bold," "Underline," "Italicize," "Cap," and "Read Paragraph." I like to keep a list of frequent commands pasted on the corner of my monitor.

Microsoft Corporation has spent a good deal of time perfecting their own *Windows Speech Recognition* (*WSR*). If you have Windows Vista, Windows 7 or 8 (but not Windows RT), *WSR* is built into the operating system. Speech recognition can be turned on by opening the Control Panel and going to Ease of Access. WSR in Windows 7 and 8 is like *Dragon NaturallySpeaking*. Windows speech recognition comes bundled free inside Windows. For best dictation results a good microphone is beneficial. I find even a $35 boom microphone, which places the microphone near your mouth, works very well.

Even though Windows and Mac OS X come with dictation, many people prefer to purchase the dictation software by Nuance. I find speech recognition very helpful. I generally speak grammatically correct sentences and I do not have to worry about spelling. With Nuance software I can use the "read paragraph or read sentence" commands to quickly review my writing.

Writing Assistive Apps

AppWriter US [iOS]

AppWriter US ($39.99) is a very good word prediction word-processing program for the iPad. As words are typed, a separate window shows possible word predictions. Select a word from this prediction window. Then the app will predict the next possible word in the sentence. *AppWriter* is very good at its predictions. Upon completion of the sentence, *AppWriter* can read back what you wrote. Within the interface, font type and color as well as background color can be adjusted. One font type is a special dyslexia font — this font is specially designed to help dyslexic individuals discriminate letters. Often dyslexic individuals do better when font color and background are different from the standard black letters on a white background. Since this is customizable within the app, you should try different font colors and background colors to see what suits you best. *AppWriter* has a built-in OCR scanner. Upload a picture, then the built-in OCR software can turn that into a typed document. The documents can then be edited or read to you. Your work and scans can be saved in *AppWriter* or transferred to Google Docs.

ClaroRead [Mac and PC]

ClaroRead is an extremely useful tool for reading and writing. The software works as a floating toolbar. If you like, you can minimize the toolbar while continuing to read or dock the toolbar to the top of your computer screen. You can read text in almost any document format. *ClaroRead* has several highlighting options. When reading within the app, you can choose the familiar sentence and word highlighting option, or there is also the "trail highlighting" option. With trail highlighting, the current word being read is highlighted while trailing words remain highlighted. I, Jim, particularly like this method. Also, within documents the font color of the sentence being read can be changed. When reading outside the application — such as with *Firefox* — select a portion of text and that will initiate the reading. While in a *Microsoft Word* document, you can read using the focus sentence feature. Only the sentence being read is highly visible because the other sentences are dimmed. You can also easily change character and line spacing within a Word document from the *ClaroRead* toolbar for easier reading. *ClaroRead* also comes with great writing features like a homophone detector, word prediction, and spell check. There is a set of excellent videos about *ClaroRead* on YouTube for you to get more information. *ClaroRead* comes in two incarnations: a basic version and a pro version. With the basic version ($99) you only can read text from outside applications. The pro version ($295) offers all the features listed above. All in all ClaroRead is an exceptional program.

Google Docs (or Google Drive)

Google offers a simplified writing suite completely online. You can make slide shows, spreadsheets, and text documents. They are available through your Gmail account. If you would rather work on your computer, you can choose to store that document on the Drive. A computer download is available that will enable you to put files into a folder on your computer and have them appear in your online Drive folder, or you can simply upload the file the old-fashioned way. Google excels in file-sharing and convenience, but as a word processor provider they are nothing special.

Handwriting with WritePad [iOS]

If writing with pen and paper is your thing, then try *WritePad* ($7.99) for the iPad. WritePad is a handwriting recognition app. Instead of paper and pen, you write on the iPad screen with your finger or a stylus. Writing with a stylus is generally much more accurate than writing with a finger. *WritePad* recognizes your handwriting and transforms it into typed text. *WritePad* is extremely accurate at identifying handwriting. The iPad's large screen offers a large writing area. After you write a few words, the program will translate them into text. Alternatively, the program offers a special writing window which covers the lower third of the iPad screen — this writing window is very handy. As you write in this window, *WritePad* quickly converts your writing into text for preview. If the preview is correct, a quick tap on an enter button adds the text to your document. *WritePad* also comes with an on-screen keyboard. When the keyboard is active, it comes with word completion. Custom document windows can have different paper colors and font types, sizes, and colors. This section was written using WritePad.

iA Writer Pro [iOS]

Writer Pro offers features that help you focus on your writing and analyze what you have written. *Writer Pro* has a simplified approach — no fancy toolbars to worry about — just the text itself. A focus mode enables the sentence you are writing or editing to stand out from the other sentences. Syntax highlighter makes parts of speech stand out for review. For example, you can select to have all verbs highlighted and then you will only see verbs with the other words faded out. You can highlight sentences, verbs, adjectives, adverbs, nouns, prepositions or conjunctions. *Writer Pro* integrates with cloud storage — iCloud or Dropbox — and also imports and exports in Word document format. It is available for both OS X ($19.99) and iOS ($9.99).

iOS 8 keyboards

iOS 8 allows additional keyboard support beyond the Apple keyboard! Now you can use third-party keyboards. Also, the Apple Keyboard itself has been improved, offering word prediction. No matter which app you are using, the keyboard gives you word predictions. Our favorite third-party keyboard is Nuance's *Swype*. Just by running your finger across the letters of the keyboard you type words. The keyboard is very good at interpreting swipes to words; it is great at correcting spelling; and it offers word predictions too. There are many other wonderful features. For under $3, it is worth it!

iWork [iOS and Mac]

iWork is Apple's comprehensive office suite: *Pages* (word processor), *Numbers* (spreadsheet) and *Keynote* (presentation). The iWork suite of programs is available for iOS and OS X. Documents sync easily between the devices with the iCloud. Admittedly, none of the programs have many accessibility features so you will want to use an accessibility app. *ClaroRead* integrates seamlessly with *Pages*. *ClaroRead* offers reading with text highlighting, spell check, word prediction, and homophone identification. iWorks utility comes in its convenience and usability, but with *ClaroRead* it can also be very handy for those with difficulty writing.

Kurzweil 3000 [Mac and PC]

Kurzweil 3000 ($1,395) is best known as a great software for reading. It also includes a word processor to assist with writing. It offers word prediction. In Jim's opinion the writing Support of *Kurzweil 3000* is weak. When he owned this software he rarely used it for writing.

MagicalPad [Mac and iOS]

MagicalPad excels in mind mapping features that will take your outline to the next level. This application is available for iOS and OS X; together both softwares cost less than $40. It uses iCloud for file sharing. Mind mapping, as a powerful outline format, encourages expressing creativity and making connections between ideas. Traditionally, mind mapping could only effectively be done with paper and pencil; that is no longer the case! With this application, texts, lists (or mini bullet-point outlines), and images can be shown on one canvas. Everything is formatable on the page, so you can have certain ideas in one color bubble and others in another color. The application is easy to use and does not require a lot of hassle in order to produce beautiful mind maps.

Microsoft Office 365 [Mac and PC, with mobile versions]

Microsoft Office 365 is a fully-featured office suite with *Word* (word processing), *Excel* (spreadsheet), *Power Point* (presentation), *One Note* (note taker), and One

Drive (cloud storage). Microsoft now offers this site as a subscription service, normally $99 a year but for students $79 for a four-year subscription. Office 365 is available for PC and Mac computers. A less featured version is available for mobile devices. Our focus here is on *Word* and One Drive. Word is the most widely used word processor on the market, certainly in business and government. Word offers more features than one generally needs, though not many accessibility features. The most useful of these are a limited word-completion feature and also a spelling and grammar check. Word can be used in conjunction with other accessibility software; for example, the *ClaroRead* toolbar integrates extremely well with Word. A full explanation of *ClaroRead* is given above. Office 365 also comes with One Drive unlimited cloud storage, which is particularly helpful for storing documents and articles.

Scrivener [Mac and PC]

Scrivener is a very powerful writing and organization application for both Mac and PC. There are four main beneficial features of this application that will help with writing and keeping research organized. One, the app organizes multiple documents into a binder system. This binder has folders or tabs and each folder/tab can hold multiple documents. As in a real binder, the documents are immediately readable and editable, contrary to a traditional digital folder system with just document thumbnail previews. These folders can be labeled different things. Thus, you can have one folder named "essay" where you keep written sections for a final essay, and another folder entitled "research" where articles and notes can be kept that will help in writing the essay. This folder and binder system helps keep everything related to the paper in one place. Two, a sophisticated search tool helps highlight and find important things within the text you are writing. More than just searching and replacing words, *Scrivener* allows you to search by formatting. This means you can find every time you use italics or made a note in red colored font. You can also search whole folders at one time. No idea or quote will escape you with this searching tool. Three, *Scrivener* supports multiple file formats. You can have your text documents right beside any pictures or videos you may use. *Scrivener* works well with *Dragon Dictation*, so you can dictate your documents right within the application. Four, my, Maria's, number one favorite feature of *Scrivener* is the brilliant appearance control. From what I can surmise there is not one color used that cannot be changed in the options menu. If you like a red background in order to stay focused, that is possible. If you want all comments in yellow, that is doable. The ability to personalize your virtual writing surface to something that makes you comfortable and feel inspired is extremely instrumental in your writing success. Moreover, specialized colored fonts make editing and idea organization easy, which also promotes good writing! *Scrivener*, a very sophisticated writing program with many tools, retails for around $50. It offers many video tutorials and a written manual to help the customer understand how to use their software.

Talking Word Processor [Mac and PC]

Talking Word Processor operates as a writing assistant in two specific ways. First, the word processor has read-aloud functionality built-in. As you type you can have each sentence read back to you or you can manually choose the amount to be read. It can be very helpful to read back a paragraph you recently wrote or, when stuck in the middle of a paragraph, to hear what has just been written to spark your next sentences. Second, there are small individual tools to help you write your best. As you type you can turn on a word prediction window. As you write, a list of predicted words, from which you can choose, will show up in a small window. You can even add words to the prediction library. When you are unsure how to spell a specific word, the prediction window will most likely show you that word before you finish typing it. Additional features include a similar word detector, dictionary, and thesaurus, all built into the toolbar of the word processor. The *Talking Word Processor* costs $99.95 or can be purchased as part of the Literacy Productivity Pack for $245.95.

Co:Writer [Mac and PC]

Co:Writer by Don Johnson is perhaps the best iOS app in this category. Don Johnson grew up as a struggling reader and writer, so he is familiar with the difficulties students face. He started a company to develop software to help dyslexic students. *Co:Writer* is exceptional at predicting the words being typed. It can correct misspelled words which follow phonetic rules or words that approximate a word meaning. For example, you might write, "C u tomaro." *Co:writer* will predict you mean "See you tomorrow." Besides having a general prediction dictionary, *Co:Writer* has over 4 million topical prediction dictionary entries — these entries include everything from biology to the American Civil War. Predicted words, written words, or sentences can be read aloud. It costs $19.99 (iOS) and is well worth the asking price.

CHAPTER 9 - Taking Notes

Taking Notes

The professor of a standard college class will lecture or demonstrate solutions to mathematic or scientific problems. You, as the student, will be expected to write notes based on this instruction for your own reference and study. In high school, the material that teachers lecture on is often a rehash of the class textbook. This is not true in college, where the professor introduces new material not in the textbook. He will touch on key concepts and terms important to the course material, which are as valuable to your understanding as the textbook itself. Write down these key terms. Later you can look them up either in your textbook or perform a Google search in order to ascertain a further explanation. Always write down anything the professor puts special attention on or specifically says, "This is important" and "This will be on the test." The professor has full right to include all material from both the textbook and his lectures on class exams. Taking diligent notes will aid you when it comes time to study for exams.

Arriving early to class is very beneficial because it gives you time to prepare for the class ahead. When I, Jim, walked to class, I would make a point to get there a few minutes early. With this extra time, I would look over my last class notes and glance at the syllabus in order to get my mind ready for this class session and new material I would soon learn. Now, if a good friend was there, I admit this prep-work went to the side. However, I did usually ask how their class assignments were going. I had a friend who would literally run from class to class to have extra time for studying. He was a straight A honors college student. That style worked for him, but it didn't suit me. I, Maria, did not "run" between classes, but I did have a reputation for being very early. I too used this time to review and catch up socially with my classmates. I found that being early helped me to calm down before class and mentally relax myself before learning new information. Also, if you missed a previous class you can use this time to seek those class notes from another student who was present. Taking the effort to be early can ensure preparedness and calmness before class.

How you conduct yourself during class matters. We are going to give you a little harsh advice. We understand that when you are in class it is tempting to check your email or text message your friends. Don't do it! Two principal reasons are: first, the professor works hard on his lectures. It shows disrespect not to be engaged and alert during them. Second, the lecture is full of very important information that will show up on the test. If you are distracted you may miss something important. Moreover, if a whole class becomes absent-minded then the professor is liable to emphasize the material of that lecture on the exam. Professors have no sympathy for students who seek guidance about information which the student himself failed to write down in the original lecture. Trust us, they know the difference between confusion and inattention on the part of the student. If you skip class or otherwise do not take notes, it is going to be hard to do well in a course.

Note Taking Styles

In-Class Notes

Here is a description of how I, Jim, take in-class notes. My method is the same whether I am handwriting them or typing them: I use my adaptation of the "Cornell Note Taking" process. You can find informative YouTube videos about this process, if you want to see a demonstration of it. First, you divide your page into four sections. Leave enough room at the top for the lecture's title and the date. Along the left hand side, draw a line about 2.5 inches from the left edge. On the bottom, leave 2 inches for a page summary. You will write your main notes in the large right hand box. Second, you start your note taking by putting the title of the lecture at the top of the page. The details of the lecture go into the large right box. I used to try to number and organize these details in an outline form, with the main points marked by a Roman numeral (I, II, III, or IV) and sub-points marked by a capital letter (A, B, or C). After my freshman year, though, I abandoned this since my points rarely coincided with the professor's outline. Instead, I used an "indentation method" of outlining, where the main points went next to the left hand line and sub-points were indented from the left. If I decided a sub-topic was a main topic, I simply drew an arrow from the indent to the left ($\leftarrow$). Lastly, when I was studying after class, I used the left hand margin space to jot down important things.

Contrarily, I could choose to place a star beside points on the right side to signify something I needed to remember. After fully reviewing, I would write a sentence or two in the bottom-section of the page, summarizing the important points to learn.

I wrote my notes in phrases not sentences. The phrases were there to help jog my memory; that is the goal of well written notes. Additionally, if I used acronyms, I made sure that I defined them somewhere on my notes. For example, I would write "CD = cell diving." For common words, I used some abbreviations: "ex = for example," "t = the," "imp = important point."

The objective is not to take perfect notes. When I got stumped or fell behind in a lecture, I would skip some space on my page, knowing that I would later fill in the blank section. Next class, I asked another student for help with that section of my notes. On the other hand, I could have listened to that part of the lecture recorded on a player or the Livescribe Smart Pen, which is discussed below, to gain the information in order to complete my notes. Also, handouts are given out in class, which often include some lecture material. If I got a handout in class, I would later join it with the class notes in my notebook.

By the time I reached graduate school, I had developed two strategies that greatly helped with taking notes. First, I read my assigned chapters before class. By reading before class, I more easily followed lectures and asked more intelligent and informed questions. Second, I supplemented my assigned readings with additional books on my subject area that were easily accessible and informative. I found these books in my university bookstore or library. For example, when I took statistics, I read a survey book by Kerlinger called *The Foundation of Behavioral Research*. The audio recording of the 4th edition is available on Learning Ally. The author's use of plain language and discussion to explain statistical concepts, rather than math formulas, appealed greatly to me. I understood statistics better due to this extra reading. Thus, I discovered that when I did this extra reading, I took fewer notes and had greater comprehension.

Textbook Notes

I, Jim, did not take many notes from books. Most of the books I read were either textbooks or books summarizing social science research. For this type of reading I highlighted in the books or ebooks. We cover highlighting in another section. Therefore, Maria will explain her method for taking notes from the books she reads:

Taking notes from a textbook or historical book is quite different from a literary book. Often we just highlight in technical books. Do so, but in addition, write down very important quotes, your impression of the author's ideas, and summary points of what you want to remember from the reading.

Since I was a Humanities major, the reading I most enjoyed was literary. I slowly devised a method to read these books and take notes at the same time. Before reading, I would ask myself what the reading was to be used for. Would I use it to talk about women, politics, miracles, etc? Answering this early on helps narrow down your focus when you read. I then thought of important points or categories for the topic of the week. I made a list of them. For example, for "women" I had points like "motherhood," "femininity," "child rearing," etc. As I read the material, I made a note beside certain sections I felt exemplified one or more of the categories I had made ahead of time. So I wrote "motherhood" beside a quote that specifically mentioned a mother or was by a mother. Later on, when I looked back on the text to find quotes or excerpts, I only needed to look at the keywords I had written in the margins rather than trying to find something in the dense text. I still use this in all my literary reading. Boiling a quote down to just one or two keywords is a wonderful exercise in minimalism and restraint.

After a course is over you might be tempted to ditch your notes from class and from the textbooks. We recommend you keep your notes! If you are planning to go to graduate school, these notes will help prepare you for advanced placement tests. Additionally, a lot of courses within a college major are related to each other, so having notes from one class might help you with another later on. Also, courses often have life application, so having your college notes may aid you later on in writing a letter or a speech. To conserve paper, choose to scan your handwritten notes for long term, eco-friendly storage.

Tools for Note Taking

Pen/Pencil and Paper

I, Jim, used to take notes with pen and paper. I especially liked the fine tip felt pens. You will be able to find a variety of pens at your university bookstore and office supply stores such as Staples or OfficeMax. I preferred to take notes in spiral notebooks; I liked the wide-line version. I would choose a different color for each class. However, some people like three-ring binders and note paper. The benefit to a three-ring binder is that you can hold handouts and notes in one place easily.

Livescribe Smart Pens

A number of students like taking notes with a Livescribe Smart Pen, a small computerized pen. You need to write in a Livescribe notebook. It can make an audio recording of the lecture while you use it to write notes. As you write, the pen matches your written notes to the audio recording. Later on, when you review your notes, touch the pen to your written notes and that portion of the lecture is played back for you. Importantly, some professors may not allow you to record the lecture. With an accommodation letter from the Students with Disabilities Office (SDS or SSD), however, the professor will permit you, specifically, to record the lecture because you have that need. The Livescribe Pen is a great aid to studying because it enables you to listen to portions of the recorded lecture based on your notes. This helps you check for accuracy and add detail to your existing notes.

Laptop Computer

A laptop can be very handy for taking notes. You will be better able to keep up with the lecture since, generally, you can type faster than you can handwrite. Some professors forbid laptops in their classes. If you especially need a laptop, have that as one of your SDS accommodations. I, Maria, cannot handwrite for long periods, so I received this accommodation. With practice you get quite used to typing full time. I learn through typing just as well as handwriting now. A courtesy you may want to consider if you are the only typist in the classroom is to have a silicone keyboard cover. The cover dramatically cuts down on keyboard sounds and helps your classmates focus on the professor rather than your keyboard.

I, Jim, found taking notes on a laptop helped me to type points listed on the whiteboard. When the professor put new terms on the board, if I were handwriting, I had to keep looking up at the word multiple times to get it down. However with a keyboard, I could just type the word looking up the entire time, saving me time and neck strain. Whenever I type notes, I still use my adapted Cornell note method. If a lecture included graphs, diagrams, or charts, I placed my drawing of them in a special notebook I kept with me for this purpose. I would give each diagram a code name or number. Then in my typed notes I would refer to diagram 'xyz' by its name or number. Thus, if you choose to type your notes you can be assured that all pertinent information will be on hand when you study.

Keep in mind, research has found several drawbacks to laptops for note taking. For example, students often type verbatim notes rather than in short key word phrases. This means that the lecture is not being processed, just transcribed; even though the notes are more complete, less is actually understood. So to combat this, type only what is necessary. Remember you won't be able to write down everything. Think before you type! Focus on writing down the main points. Today, most professors lecture from PowerPoint slides. Do not type out the whole slide, just the crucial parts. Ask the professor if he will post them online or allow you a copy of them as an SDS accommodation. Let these slides help you recognize what is important as you listen to the lecture. Additionally, if the professor is reviewing things you know or things in the textbook, simply jot down a note to review that concept from the book rather than type out what he says verbatim. Use the time you save typing to think more carefully about what you are actually noting down.

CHAPTER 9 - Foreign Language Study

Taking a foreign language can seem daunting. An already difficult subject becomes more difficult with dyslexia. Remembering vocabulary words is especially time consuming and hard. Grammatical features in a sentence, so obvious to others, seem to vanish or be invisible. Lastly, translating overwhelms the mind because so much has to be considered at one time. I, Maria, have struggled with some of this but I also found ways to excel in foreign language classes. I have completed coursework in Latin and French. My success derived from specific study skills that enabled me to own and use the material I learned. I want to share with you now my techniques.

As I learned Latin, for example, there were three elements I had to grapple with constantly: vocabulary, grammar, and translation. I needed to master the first two in order to properly complete my translations. Of course, I made plenty of mistakes in my translation and grammar, but I worked hard to get better and better. I will say this now, that I had to put in many, many hours to do well and had to dramatically overcompensate to maintain high grades. Often dyslexics work harder than other students and the true hard work necessary to learn a foreign language serves as a great example of this. Assuredly though, the work-ethic and self-confidence which blossom out of long hours of studying are truly one of life's treasures!

Vocabulary

Vocabulary sits at the heart of any language. Reading or listening to a foreign language requires recognition of words. The ability to recognize foreign words may take more time for dyslexic students. Using that time wisely helps make the words stick better and longer. Split the time into two phases: first, connect with the foreign word and second, employ specific techniques to cement that word into the mind.

When you learn words as a child, often someone shows representative pictures or uses synonyms to describe them. Learning foreign words at any age can operate in the same fashion. When you learn the word for "window" in French (*fenêtre*) put that word on a sticky note and stick it on your window. The connection made between object and word helps the word itself to stick in your mind. Similarly, make connections with synonyms. When you learn the Latin word for "to strike down" (*occidere*), recall synonyms to help you remember the meaning of the word and the word itself. Forming these word associations with another word or object enables you to think about one thing and conjure up a thought about another. Remembering a picture or simpler word may be easier and help you recall the foreign word you intended.

Other ways to connect with foreign words include using other associations — such as with English derivatives — and rhythmic reminders. I have a silly way to remember the Latin adverb *tandem*, meaning "at last." I always say to myself "at last I can sky-dive in tandem" and then I instantly remember. A more serious and effective association would be to connect foreign words with their English derivatives: for example, the French word *chaise* becomes the English word *chair*.

Rhythmic memory taps into your own ability to form and recognize patterns, both oral and visual. For example, when I needed to remember the meaning of the Latin word *subito* I just clapped loudly. That "sudden" sound would help jog my memory and illuminate the meaning of the word to me. Finding a beat to the word or remembering the key strokes to type are other rhythmic clues to recall words.

After you connect with a word you must practice your recall to truly memorize it. Using flash cards best cements vocabulary memorization. There are different ways to use flash cards, though, other than just flashing the card and repeating the translation. Flash cards can be made by hand, but there are also websites that help you make digital flash cards. My favorite is Quizlet and Brainscape. Here follow a few ways to practice recalling foreign words:

1. Traditional flash cards are very effective in the beginning stages of memorization. First, flash the foreign word and say the English meaning. Then reverse it. Flash the English word and say the foreign meaning. Then shuffle your cards, maybe even have some with English on front and others with foreign words.

2. After you memorize the words this way move onto spelling. Flash the foreign word and spell out the English meaning; this forces you to be very accurate in your English translation. Then flash the English word and spell out the foreign word. For me this was always the hardest step. Take the time to master this step. Remember that on your test you will need to write foreign words, so practicing early helps you to excel in spelling the foreign words on the test. Quizlet allows you to do this right within their website or mobile app.

3. Find a paragraph from your homework that includes a lot of the new vocabulary words. Work to recognize them as you read the paragraph.

Each of these three steps helped me to stay in the position where I had to recall the word over and over. Sometimes we just go through the motions when using flash cards, but if you also write out the word and read it in a paragraph then you will know that you *know* the word! Also, taking the time to do these steps ensures that you have seen the word enough times to lock it in your memory.

Grammar

Most individuals, myself included, take English grammar for granted while talking and reading. I just assume that my audience knows "indirect statements" and "relative clauses" well enough to follow me. When learning a foreign language every tiny aspect of grammar becomes aloof and strange. After the first few weeks the strain to understand lessens and clarity comes, but soon many grammatical concepts crowd themselves and compete for attention in your mind. You must have an accurate and firm understanding of the grammar you are learning to counter-attack the encroaching confusion. This is accomplished through practice, studying, and even sometimes tutoring. Here I want to suggest ways to study grammar and retrieve concepts from your textbooks.

When we first learn a language we often read English and the foreign language together, jumping between the two languages to find the meaning of the sentence. The English serves as a brace or guide in the beginning to give crucial clues to what the foreign words say. Moreover, the English translations ground the foreign passage in terms and ideas with which we are already familiar. This support system can be further evolved into how we study the grammatical concepts themselves. Transform the dense textbook explanation into your own English words and then you can understand it. Rewording the definition with your own words will unlock the box to truly comprehend and remember grammatical concepts!

Neither you (I assume) nor I are grammarians so I do not want you to feel unduly burdened by my above proposition that you write your own grammar definitions. I suggest that a well-worded study guide, relying heavily on the original material, will serve you better than simply highlighting your book or trying to regurgitate only what the professor says. Writing your own study guide is taking an active part in your effort to commandeer foreign grammar concepts.

Here are my goals whenever I write a Grammar study guide:
1. Cover all the material that will appear on the upcoming test and had been on previous tests.
2. Give preferential treatment to conceptual information given by the professor, making sure to include it where appropriate.
3. If a test-prep packet is provided, include all grammatical concepts held therein.
4. Explain concepts as economically as possible.
5. Collapse the countless sentences exemplifying various grammatical concepts from the textbook and homework into just one or two for the study guide.
6. Organize concepts how they best make sense to me, rather than just chapter-by-chapter based on the textbook.
7. Keep the study guide short, knowing the length reflects how much must be memorized.

There are different ways to organize the information you collect, here are a few suggestions:
• By syntactical element: Verbs, Nouns, Adjectives, Adverbs, Prepositions, Conjunctions, and Interjections.
• By physical layout: Split the page in half and keep definitions on one side and examples on the other.
• By color: Highlight definitions in one color, foreign examples in another, and English examples in yet another.
• By test/chapter: Flow the study guide exactly as the class has flowed, keeping everything in the order learned.

All the effort expounded in writing this study guide pays dividends. The act of writing or typing information helps to cement it. Time spent organizing the grammatical concepts helps the ideas sink in. No matter how difficult the grammar, actively engaging and working with it will help you succeed in learning it.

Translation
Translating can be intimidating. You must remember vocabulary and identify the grammatical function of every word in the sentence. Rewriting the sentence correctly into English from the original foreign text remains the goal, but a lot of work has to be put into accomplishing that goal. Your professor and diligent practice can propel you to successful translations. However, when I translate, I find, despite my skills and knowledge, I get very confused — lost even — and I tend to lose words, not

remembering if I had translated them or not. Staying organized and noting the information for each word assure me that I won't get confused. I provide here an example of what I mean; this can be written by hand or typed.

Original: amat
Grammar: 3rd Person Singular Present (*amo, amare*)
Rough Translation: to love
Final Translation: he/she/it loves

The more you put on paper, fewer thoughts have to circle around in your mind. Referencing the grammatical information aids in a correct translation. Translations offer the opportunity to showcase all that you know. Properly writing down that knowledge helps keep everything sorted and prevents confusion and encourages your best translation to shine.

Completing foreign language coursework comes with many challenges. Preparing and studying counteract the difficulties and ensure success! I hope these small suggestions can help you on your way to success in foreign language classes.

CHAPTER 10 - Tips for Studying

Learning Styles

Everyone has different learning and studying styles. Discovering your learning style and the strengths attached to it will help you be a wonderful learner. Educational researchers have identified three different learning styles: visual, auditory, and kinesthetic. Here are two web-links to tests to help you determine your learning style: learning style inventory and VARK Questionnaire. Do not be surprised if you learn that you have strengths in more than one learning modality because, in fact, combining two or more modalities will strengthen your learning. We have some examples below.

Besides just the three main types above, there is a further specification between global (big picture) or linear (details) learners. Global learners like to have the big picture of a subject, chapter, or lecture. They appreciate an overall theory first and then want to go back to put details into that theory. Whereas, linear learners like to immerse themselves in the details and let those details generate the overall theme, such as of a class lecture or chapter.

Everyone has a learning style, but Ben Foss, the author of *Dyslexia Empowerment Plan*, has developed an inventory of eight strengths specialized to dyslexic learners. The strengths assessment test shows the student's strengths in the areas of: verbal, social, narrative, spatial, kinesthetic, visual, mathematical/ scientific, and musical. I, Jim, scored highest in musical, verbal, and mathematical strengths. This explains why I like to give lectures and want to sing to audiences. I, Maria, placed highest in visual, verbal, and social strengths. Thus, I enjoy re-presenting information in my own visual outlines and I am also comfortable talking to large groups of people.

When I, Jim, took the assessment for my learning style, I found out I am an auditory and kinesthetic learner. As an auditory and kinesthetic learner I like to listen to lectures and, when trying to learn material, I often prefer to repeatedly handwrite the items I am learning. For example, to learn foreign vocabulary, I would take a sheet of paper and divide it down the middle. I then write the English words on one side and the foreign ones on the other side. I then write down the words as I say them aloud. Another example, when I prepare for an essay test, I write out bullet points about the subject of the test and then practice by repeatedly writing them down, in order to memorize them. Immediately when I begin the test, I flip my test paper over and write out those points that I had memorized. Last example, I excel in explaining concepts to other people; in doing so I orally cement the ideas in my mind. In addition to being an auditory and kinesthetic learner, I am also a global learner. I prefer to get the big picture before memorizing the details. Hence, I read a chapter over to get the big picture before analyzing the details of that chapter.

I, Maria, am a visual and auditory learner. I feed off being able to "see" concepts and keep things visually organized. Whenever I listen to a lecture or watch a video I always want to capture that information again in a visual outline of my own making. I think very much in pictures and often color-code emotions or thoughts in my mind. On the other hand, I can process verbal information and remember information given in lectures or conversations well. In addition to all of this I am a linear (or detail-based) learner. I like to find patterns based on a lot of details and small examples. This translates into my ability to create very detailed notes before I start writing a paper. However, sometimes I struggle to see the big picture or capture it in words due to my over zealous compulsion to look at the details within that large concept.

Staying Organized

While in college, managing your time is important — in fact, doing so well is a skill you need to acquire. Let's say you take four classes with each one meeting three times per week, so you are in class twelve hours. What are you going to do with all that extra time? Study, of course! The rule of thumb is for every hour in class, students are expected to spend two hours studying outside of class. In our example, that would mean thirty-six hours studying a week. You will have to judge for yourself how much time you schedule and how that reflects in your grades. Your goal grade will also be a factor in this decision. One of the realities of dyslexia is that it will most likely take you longer to read and study things than students without that limitation — this was very true for both of us!

At the beginning of every semester the professor will provide you a syllabus for their course. The syllabus will indicate chapters to be read, assignments to be submitted, and dates for tests (very often in college there are midterm and final exams within the semester). If you take several classes, use a calendar to keep the different class timelines straight. I, Jim, used to keep a notebook for each class with a copy of the syllabus at the beginning of the notebook. However digital may be better for you — I know that I had a very difficult time maintaining a calendar until I got an iPhone with its iCalendar app. Now I sync all my events on my phone. Since my smart phone is always with me, my calendar is always handy! I, Maria, have used paper calendars and e-calendars. I prefer a digital record because then I can get notifications on my phone before something is due or a test. I like to take it one step further and have a separate digital calendar just for school or even use a separate school calendar app, such as *iStudiez*. Either way, you should make it a practice to look at each subject and it's adjoining calendar events once a day to plan your study time. Planning your study time should include making a to-do list for that day of things you want to accomplish. Don't forget that your time between classes can also count as study time. If you use some of that time, like we did, then you have more free hours later in the day to participate in sports or practice music.

Thinking About Studying

As many options as there are for study time, there are an equal number for study space. Some prefer their dorm room with music playing, while others like the quiet of the college library. I, Jim, always preferred the library because there were fewer distractions. Since my textbooks were available as audio files, I would put on my headphones and listen to my books while following along in the print textbook. Sometimes the boredom of the library, though, put my mind on autopilot. So at times I enjoyed studying at the student union where I could have a coke and chips and enjoy the hustle and bustle around me. If I was sleepy I learned to take ten minute naps to rejuvenate myself. Other than snoozing, I found getting up and walking around during a ten minute break was preferable to sitting in the same spot, even if I was phoning a friend (when you get up to walk around do not leave something valuable around like your computer). I, Maria, prefer to study in the comfort of my own home (or dorm room). I do not like moving my stuff constantly nor people walking and whispering around me. I like to drink tea and have some music on speaker occasionally. A particular study space may not be as crucial to you — you may be more flexible — but finding your ideal study place is vital because it is one more thing which will help you be comfortable and productive when you study.

While you consider your study plan and space, also remember to minimize your distractions. Limit your internet surfing on sites like Facebook and Readit and text messaging while you study. Many students today feel they are great at multitasking — texting while reading that chapter for biology. Research studies have shown this is not the case. These tasks conflict with each other; reading comprehension is lower if combined with other tasks like texting.

Let your friends know that you will be available in an hour to respond to texts, then put away your phone. (If you use your phone for music or audiobooks put it on "airplane mode" or "do not disturb" to restrict the flow of new text messages and Twitter notifications.) After that hour, take a ten minute networking break to text back whomever you want and then settle down for another fifty minutes of studying.

It is important to change the subject you are studying every fifty minutes. Our minds get fatigued and bored with the same subject for too many hours. Variety keeps your mind keen and ready to learn. Further, if practiced correctly then you will evenly space out the time you spend with new vocabulary, ideas, and concepts, which will help them get into your long term memory better. This is called "the principle of spaced practice." Spaced practice literally builds stronger neural connections in our brains than would be created with a single massive practice. That is why cramming for an exam may help you pass a test, but a day later you won't remember what you crammed for.

In college there are about four different types of homework: reading your assigned book, working out math or science problems, completing written assignments, and studying for quizzes and tests. Sometimes you may have a creative project that requires you to make something. How you approach these different types of homework matters to your success, so let's break them down, excluding the creative project.

Having to read the assigned text was never easy for me, Maria. However, there is a two-fold approach to accomplishing this well. One, please refer to our section on reading where we talk about book structures, reading strategies, and technological assistance. Two, take a moment to think about the size of your reading assignment and plan accordingly. Consider how long it will take to finish the reading. If it will be longer than an hour then see if you can break up the reading over several days or times within a day (remember, ideally you should change subjects every hour). Think about what time of day is best to do the reading. The sharper or more awake you are when you read, the more you will remember ultimately. When you sit down to read, have something nearby to write notes on. All of this boils down to being deliberate when you decide to read an assigned book; think before you read!

Finishing math/science homework and written assignments can follow the same advice. Simply, break it up into smaller pieces/steps and make time for re-drafts or checking your answers. Writing can easily become very overwhelming and seem impossible. If you take the time, though, to do it a little every day or at least every few days over the course of the week or semester then everything scary about writing will cease. Moreover, break up your writing into steps. For example, step 1) roughly sketch ideas, step 2) write outline, and step 3) slowly fill in outline with your own amazing full sentences. Please, make sure to have a first draft complete 1 to 3 days before the assignment is due. This will allow you the time to edit and revise what you wrote. Being able to re-read your writing will give you fresh perspective on content and the ability to see mistakes. Trying to finish a writing assignment the night before only leads to problems, but properly scheduling your time will lead to wonderful results!

Lastly, you will need to study for tests and quizzes. Studying is a very personal venture. The more you study the more you figure out what works for you. Some people love to create sticky notes or flash cards; others read their highlights; and still others re-read their assigned texts. I, Maria, will offer you my personal story of my best studying experience, which I had during Human Biology.

I am not a scientifically gifted person, so I really had to buckle down to do well in that class. The professor would lecture and show a powerpoint each class. While in class I only wrote down things that the professor said which were not on the powerpoint. At home, I took the professor's powerpoint and converted it into a Word document. I then added my in-class notes to that document, integrating my notes with the professor's powerpoint information. I colored my notes to keep them distinguished from the powerpoint information. Before I knew it I had a study guide. A few days before the test I began to read once a day through the study guide for the chapters to be covered on the test. By the end, I had gone through the material many times and was ready to be tested on it. I got 100 on the test!

Study Help

Most colleges offer free tutoring centers — which provide help to students in math, writing, science, and foreign language. It is important to contact the tutoring centers early if you are struggling in a subject. They can help you with assignments, studying for a test, and developing strategies for studying. Additionally, science and math classes often offer extra help via non-mandatory lab or review sessions. I, Jim, found it especially helpful to attend these sessions.

One time I was tutoring a student in statistics. After several weeks of tutoring, this student informed me that he withdrew from the course and changed his major since he did not like math classes. He felt like he let me down. I told him it was just fine and that we go to college in order to find out what we like and what we want to study. Thus, tutors can help you get through a class and be there when you learn for yourself what you like.

Accepting help when you are struggling can be difficult. Even if you know it will work, it still seems embarrassing. If other students knew, they might think of you differently or even think worse of you. Just telling you that this is not the case may not convince you. Talking with a friend or loved one may help you feel more comfortable with the idea of getting help. Here, though, we would like to offer one rationalization that may aid you. Whenever you start a new class, you do not feel bad that you do not already know the material. You seek the teacher and their ability to impart knowledge to you. Sadly, sometimes the class session is not long enough or the teacher may not have that special something to help you understand the material. In this case you can either accept this or change it by seeking additional instruction from a tutor. The tutor is there to help supplement your in-class learning and aid you in making bridges of understanding where you may have confusion. So, just as you would not be ashamed to learn new things from a class professor, you should not be ashamed to learn more from a tutor offering you a supplement to your class.

Sometimes it is best to study alone but, at other times, with a friend or in a group. When I, Jim, first went to college I was not used to sitting and studying for long hours. I was up out of my seat every fifteen minutes. With that level of distraction it was hard to get things done. Fortunately, I made friends with Dave, who was a straight A student. I would go to the library with him at night, Sunday through Thursday. Simply, I sat at the same table with him studying. He rarely took breaks and studied straight for four hours. He changed subjects every hour. My goal became to emulate Dave as much as I could. Slowly over several months, I began to be able to sit for at least fifty minutes, making sure to take a ten minute break and change subjects every hour. Also, Dave showed me how to highlight just the important points in a chapter, rather than almost the whole thing. My study time with Dave was one of the components that changed me from a C student to an A student.

If you opt for a study group proper, figure out soon the group's level of preparedness and commitment. You want to study with other hard working students. A good study group can help motivate you to study a difficult subject. Also, if there is too much for one person to review, different members of the group can each create different parts of the ultimate study guide — i.e. divide and conquer! On the other hand, students who are happy with a minimal grade usually read through their notes once, congratulate themselves on how much they know, and then are not willing to study further. So if you are in a group with this type of student, either look for another group or go to the tutoring center for help.

Staying Active

You may be asking yourself, "What should I do other than study?" Other activities squeezing their way into your schedule are important. There are two major reasons: (1) Our brains need a variety of activities to run optimally. (2) We need to get our minds off of school work; social interaction can do that. School may be "number one" but you need a number two and three to be a well-balanced person.

Participation in intramural sports can keep you physically active and socially engaged. You could also exercise in a gym three to four times a week. Most college campuses have gym facilities available to students. This is the perfect opportunity to learn Yoga or take Zumba for the first time.

If you are not the athletic type, then consider student organizations or volunteer work. I, Maria, remained very active with student organizations while in college. That allowed me both to socialize and feel like I was giving back to the University. You can also choose to leave your campus altogether by volunteering at a local hospital or church.

These activities have many benefits. In addition to keeping you physically and mentally healthy, they also grow your resume. We assure you that hours spent volunteering, playing or leading sports, and joining a student organization will pay dividends when you need to show your civic engagement and potential leadership experience. So with so many benefits why not join!

When not studying, try sleeping. Research shows that our brains are actually at work while we are asleep. Neuroscientists have demonstrated that the brain integrates what we have been studying into long-term memories while we are sleeping. So sleep is actually important to learning.

Technological Assistance for Studying

Notability [iOS and Mac]

Notability is a note-taking app, able to capture oral, handwritten, and typed notes. By writing on the iPad screen, either with your finger or a stylus, you add handwritten notes. A pop-up window at the bottom of the screen (or top for left handers) enables you to write in large cursive, which is converted into smaller readable notes. A pop-up keyboard allows for typed notes. While writing in the way most comfortable for you, *Notability* can simultaneously make a recording of a lecture or a meeting. For $2.99 in the iOS App Store and $9.99 in the OS X App Store, *Notability* is worth getting.

iStudiez Pro [iOS]

iStudiez Pro empowers students to remain organized. You can schedule assignments, exams, and weekly class meets per class within one convenient App. Notifications can be shown for any of these so you won't forget any assignment or test. It keeps classes color coded so you will not confuse assignments or exams between different classes. With the iOS and OS X version you can sync information through the iCloud. This app offers a central location for all things school and automatically does some things that would take time and effort manually on a traditional calendar.

eCalendar

Today e-calendars are not hard to find or use. You can put in events taking place in the past, present, and future and have notifications pop-up or emailed to you. You can make several calendars distinguishing all the facets of your life, not to mention personalize the calendars' color and name. Along with pre-installed calendars, you may choose to use an internet-based calendar, such as Google Calendar. This one is particularly handy for sharing with others or easily syncing across devices.

Other Products

Please see other sections for suggestions on reading and writing software that may also make a difference in your studying.

Conclusion

All of these are just a few of our suggestions about how to organize your learning and studying. We recommend that you take a study skills course or workshop in college if you did not have one in high school. Another option is to read several study skills books that are available from bookshare.org. As you develop your study approach, your classes will become more manageable and you will get more out of them.

CHAPTER 11 - Social Life

One great thing about college is the opportunities for social life and social activities. There are football games to go to, clubs to join, and musical groups to perform with. All-in-all college offers endless opportunities for fun. A healthy, balanced college social life offers three main benefits: friends, expression of creativity, and release from the academic strain. Believe it or not, staying socially active remains a key element to your academic success.

One of the first places you may meet people is in your dorm. Sometimes roommates become good friends, but quite often, they find that they do not have a lot in common or clash personalities. So, if you and your roommate do not immediately bond, do not worry because you will find friends on campus. You can meet people in the dining areas, in class, at the college recreation center, and at the student center. It is up to you how open you are with the people you meet, but never fear, an opportunity will come to make new friends.

Joining clubs or performance groups is a wonderful way to meet people and maintain consistent social involvement. I, Jim, loved to sing, so I participated in the college choir and men's glee club. I not only earned benefits for participating but I was able to go on a two-week tour with the glee club, which was great fun. I, Maria, remained a part of student organizations throughout my undergraduate time. I was part of an honors society, Christian club, and my department's student organization, of which I even became president. I loved being a part of these organizations because I stayed active and engaged with individuals and events happening on campus.

The variety of organizations differs greatly based on the college you go to. A large university will have innumerable student organizations, whereas a community college may have just a few. There is also a wide range of organization types, from religious to academic-merit-based. To learn more about these types and which ones you want to join, contact your future college student center. Most colleges have an office dedicated to helping freshman or transfer students assimilate into the college. They are there to help guide you to find that organization which is perfect for you. On the other hand, you can talk to your academic adviser, who may suggest academic student organizations. These clubs can benefit you in your education and professional track as well as put you with like-minded students. The opportunities are endless, so have faith that there is somewhere just right for you!

You may be athletically gifted, in which case you may want to join a sports team. At university there are two choices: leagues and intramural. You would need to try out to be in a league; however, intramural games are available to all. In addition to sports, often large universities have a recreation center with a fully equipped gym. There you can use the equipment (including a pool) or take a class, such as Zumba or Yoga.

You could easily spend all your time just having fun, but also keep your main objective in mind: an education! I, Jim, wanted to join a fraternity in college. After looking around, nothing seemed to suit me. A professor gave me some very good advice. He said, "Keep in mind the importance of your education. Four years from now a fraternity will not be a lasting element in your life. Your Education will last." I did join the music fraternity Phi Mu Alpha, an academic and social fraternity. Looking back, my professor's advice was very true: now that years have passed I see my education is what has lasted.

Sometimes college is where we learn that we have personal challenges. If you experience this, you can seek the free counseling services which are found at most colleges. Such counseling often provides a good opportunity to know yourself better. It is also a good way to overcome feelings of helplessness and to build your self-esteem. Your sessions are private — in other words they do not report to your parents or friends — so feel free to take advantage of these services.

Appendix - Jim and Maria Discuss Reading Styles

Within an email exchange, Maria shared with me, Jim, that she had read 80 books in 2014. She read 71 of these after she started using audio-supported reading (especially text-to-speech) with her iPad or Kindle Fire. Thus, Maria read with abundance once she was properly equipped! Here is a partial list of some of Maria's reading:
• Murder She Wrote: Murder on the QE2 - Donald Bain
• The Two Lives of Charlemagne - (trans) Lewis Thorpe
• Phantom of the Opera - Gaston Leroux
• Late Antiquity a Very Short Introduction - Gillian Clark
• Around the World in 80 Days - Jules Verne
• Jane Eyre - Charlotte Bronte
• Pride and Prejudice - Jane Austin
• Bible Promises for the Graduate - Karen Moore
• The Time Machine - H. G. Wells
• Dracula - Bram Stoker
• The Nibelungenlied - (trans.) A. T. Hatto
• Heidi - Johanna Spyri
• A Christmas Carol - Charles Dickens

• The Hobbit and The Lord of the Rings - J.R.R. Tolkien

This is just a small sample of Maria's list. Wow, 80 books!!! I looked over Maria's list and was very impressed; what fun! Maybe, I read 15 books in a year. Those were the days when I scanned books and turned them into audiobooks. I loved the variety of things Maria read. I read mostly nonfiction, but since I need some relaxing time in the evenings, I'm thinking about picking up some fiction. One can only spend so much time of the day with things that are mentally challenging. I read mostly during the day and I get about an equal amount of ebooks from Bookshare and Amazon Kindle Store.

Maria replied to me that I now knew about her passion for murder mysteries. In the past Maria spent a lot of time watching TV mysteries: Murder She Wrote, Diagnosis Murder, Poirot, Matlock, Columbo, Monk, etc. Maria now carries her interests into reading mystery books. For Maria, watching or reading murder mysteries serve as a great mental exercise. She says, "I do not watch anything gory; I prefer figuring out the pieces and following the mental track of the investigator rather than the crime itself. Murder mysteries takes up a lot of my pleasure reading." Maria would like to ultimately be a literary historian, so most of her non-mystery, pleasure fiction reading — such as the classics Jane Eyre, Dracula, Time Machine, etc. — actually help her to acquire wider knowledge and sharpen her analytic skills. She says, "I am just lucky that my 'work' is also quite fun." Maria likes to read during the day, especially the morning. She has never been able to go to sleep reading.

Here follows an edited transcript of the rest of our conversation, where we discuss our most personal experiences with daily audio-supported reading:

Maria -

I am — like you, Mr. Jim — 50/50 Bookshare and Amazon for ebooks. Amazon offers a wonderful ebook selection and the Amazon Cloud. I love the Cloud because I can open books (with all my highlights) on my computer, iPad, or Kindle. Bookshare also provides a substantial ebook library. I just take issue that the footnotes of the Bookshare ebooks are not linked in the book, so, with the addition of inconsistent tables of contents, footnotes are very difficult to access.

I especially appreciate that Amazon and Bookshare ebooks can be read with a synthetic voice (no independent audiobook required). I have become quite accustomed to the synthetic voices and have even come to prefer them. I like the speed control, the accuracy, and consistent voice pitch. Thus, I too prefer Bookshare/Kindle to Learning Alley. I like to use audiobooks only for difficult or pleasureful reads. I also employ them when I know the text will contain a lot of foreign language passages or difficult words, all of which the synthetic voice can mess up.

When I read with a synthetic voice or audiobook, speed control is really important to me. On the Kindle Fire, I maintain 3x/4x speed, unless it is a particularly difficult text. On Audible, I like to go up to 2x/3x. On VoiceDream, I vary between 400-700 wpm. I read much better if the audio goes really fast; that way I do not get bored or mentally side-tracked. Some people think such speeds are crazy, but it works really well for me.

Jim -

When I was in graduate school, I used a special tape-recorder which allowed me to speed up the audio-track, but in those days doing so made the voices sound like the chipmunks. Later on, they came out with tape-recorders that adjusted for voice pitch when speeding up the voice. Nowadays, it's all automatically adjusted. In Voice Dream, I generally read at about 225 wpm. On the Kindle, I read at 1.5x. I wish the Kindle had a 1.25x. On Audible, I read at 1-1.25x. Since almost all of my undergraduate and graduate school reading was done by students reading to me or Learning Ally recorded books, I got used to hearing people read at the regular rate of speech. However, you, Maria, have encouraged me to try fast speeds, which I am now experimenting with.

Maria -

I think you, Mr. Jim, are a lot more patient than I am. It makes sense that you got used to the regular human reading rate due to being read to so much. I just know that I have difficulty staying focused when there is too much time between words. I learned this about myself gradually. I once had a class where the professor kept over-emphasizing how fast they talked and how hard it might be to follow them. I remember clearly being half way into that semester and wondering when this "speed" was going to come out because I found the lecture to be at quite a reasonable pace. At the end of one class another student came up to me and said how overwhelmed they were due to the sheer speed of the professor's talking. I learned something about myself that day. I guess it has gotten exaggerated even more now with this fast reading. I do not do it to "show off," I am just grateful I live in an age where 300-700 wpm does not sound like a chipmunk!

To answer your question about which synthetic voices I prefer, I like the Ivona text-to-speech voices — Salli, Joey, and Amy. Whenever these voices come to OS X, I am going to buy them immediately and replace "Alex" for good! Reading on Kindle or iPad, I use a very specific system to optimize my use of voices. Whenever I read for pleasure, non-school related, I use Salli. She actually sounds surprisingly like me and it makes me feel as if I am just reading on my own (only I am not of course). I think there is something to be said about hearing material read by a synthetic voice of your same gender. When I read scholarly material or an important literary text, I use Joey. The difference and deepness of the voice gives me the mental cue that I need to focus more. Lastly, in order not to get tired of the voices or to start tuning them out, I occasionally use Amy (or "Tracy" of Acapela) to spice up the sound and keep my reading fresh and focused.

Jim —

Over the years my preferences of text-to-speech voices have changed as different voices were developed. I liked the AT&T voices Crystal and Paul for a long time. Then the William voice. I now use the Joey voice, which is on the Kindle and available with Voice Dream Reader. I prefer to use male voices. When text-to-speech voices first came out, they were very robotic and mechanical sounding. Today, though, these voices sound just like a regular person. Like you, Maria, I prefer the new text-to-speech voices to listening to most people reading except for professional audiobook narration.

Before there were ebooks, I read a lot of audiobooks through the National Library Services For the Blind and Physically Handicapped (NLS). Since there is a limited number of audiobooks on technology in their library, I read a wide variety of books: mostly science and mystery. With ebooks I like to read about the following topics:
• how technology affects society
• how economics is changing in countries around the world
• the history of books and the reading process

• how to teach reading
• dyslexia
• how books and reading changed society

Here are some titles I've read:
• The Experience Economy
• What's Mine Is Yours: The Rise of Collaborative Consumption
• Wikinomics
• Robots Will Steal Your Job But That's Ok
• Zero Marginal Cost Society
• Free the Future of a Radical Price
• Race Against the Machine
• The Second Machine Age
• Gutenberg the Geek
• The Book in the Renaissance
• The Read Aloud Handbook
• 99 Ways To Get Kids To Love Reading
• 99 Ways To Get Kids To Love Writing
• Overcoming Dyslexia
• Early Reading Instruction
• The Fluent Reader
• To Heaven and Back

Maria —
    When I first discovered Learning Alley, I was eager to try it out. That summer (2013) I needed to read a book called *Rise of Western Christendom*. This book was

available through Learning Alley. So I got the physical book from the library and set up the audio. Not adjusting the speed, I just began to go through the text. I noticed that, although I was mostly understanding what I was reading, I was having a very hard time physically following along with the audio. The book had small print and was quite physically large and I was not able to use a cursor (using my finger or a pen is too difficult for me) on the text. Fast-forwarding to the summer of 2014, I learned that if I made the text very large on the digital screen, then there would be few enough words to deal with at one time. Thus, I could follow the words no matter what the audio-reading speed.

One thing I am not able to do is just listen to text without the physical words in front of me. I have a good auditory memory and processor, but sometimes I cannot understand the word being said. When I listen, things can easily sound garbled (literally like gibberish) and then I can't think of what the right word is. So I like to have the text itself in front of me. When I watch television, I always keep the closed captioning on so that I don't miss something that's being said. When I am in class I concentrate extremely hard so that I understand everything.

Jim —

When I read at high speeds, I cannot follow the words. I loose track of where I am on the page, so, often, I simply just listen without looking at the text.

Closing Note

Both of us are members of the National Library Services (NLS) . One can get a large number of audiobooks and audio magazines from NLS. If you are dyslexic, you have to get a physician's signature on the application form stating that your reading limitation is neurologically-based. For dyslexics this is true, since dyslexia is a neurologically-based reading difference. We highly recommend joining the NLS.

Acknowledgements

I, Jim, wish to thank my co-author, Maria Johnson. It has been a pure joy writing and collaborating with her. Maria's enthusiasm and insights about going through college are reflected throughout this book. I wish to also thank Linda Nuttall, my loving wife. She is a mainstay in my life. She helps me with the little and big things in life on a daily based.

I, Maria, would like to the thank Mr. Jim. He has not only given me the opportunity to co-write this, but also been an incredible encourager. I am deeply indebted to my loving parents for their support and help. Additionally, I thank the teachers and educational administrators that have made an immense difference in my success.

Made in the USA
Monee, IL
20 May 2022

96757523R00103